The changing

Role and Status of Women

during the 20th century

Colin P. F. Hughes, Catrin Stevens and R. Paul Evans

The changing Role and Status of Women during the 20th century

© Aberystwyth University, 2012

Published by CAA, Aberystwyth University, Gogerddan Mansion, Aberystwyth, Ceredigion, SY23 3EB (www.aber.ac.uk/caa)
Sponsored by the Welsh Government.

ISBN: 978-1-84521-441-8

Editor: Lynwen Rees Jones
Designer: Richard Huw Pritchard
Source research and copyright clearing: Gwenda Lloyd Wallace
Printed by: Cambrian Printers

The publisher would like to thank:
The Monitoring Panel: Jean-Marc Alter, Neil Evans, Carole Bryan-Jones, Meinir Jones and Christian Rees, for their valuable guidance.

St Brigid's School, Denbigh; Cyfarthfa High School, Merthyr Tydfil; Ysgol Aberconwy, Conwy for taking part in the trialling process.

Gareth Holt for providing the examination practice sections for chapters 1-6.

Thank you to the following for kind permission to reproduce illustrations:

Getty Images: pp. 2, 17(r), 24(b), 30(l), 113

© National Museum of Wales: pp. 3(t,r), 5(t,r), 47(b), 50(b,r)

West Glamorgan Archive Service: p. 4(t)(P/PR/47/4/14)

The National Archives: p. 6(b)(COPY1/278 (99)), 56(t)

© National Trust Images: p. 7(b)

South Tyneside Council: p. 10(b,r)

Alpha Press Agency Ltd./The People's History Museum: p. 11(c)

Courtesy of Baroness Kinnock of Holyhead: p. 11(b,r)

Mirrorpix/British Cartoon Archive: p. 16(t)

Topfoto: pp. 17(l), 33(b,r), 40, 41(l), 60, 77, 78, 79(t,l and b,r), 80(t,r), 81, 83(t), 84(l), 85, 94(b), 96(b,l), 99(l), 100(l), 106(t,r), 108(t,l), 109(t), 110(b), 114(b,r), 119, 120(b,r), 123, 125, 128(b), 129(t and b), 130(t and c), 132(t)

National Library of Wales: pp. 19(t)(from *Maternity and Child Welfare, The Official Organ of the Central Council for Infant and Child Welfare*, No. 116, Vol. X, No. 8, (London: John Bale, Sons & Danielsson, Ltd., August 1926) p. 254); 57(t,l) (GCC03740), 98(D.A. Thomas Papers), 102(l)(PG2368/20)

Hackney Museum: p. 20(b)

Central Manchester University Hospitals NHS Foundation Trust: p. 21(t)

Mary Evans Picture Library: pp. 24(t), 90(r), 92(b), 97(b), 107(b)

Merched y Wawr: pp. 28, 39(b,r), 46(b,r), 53(r), 62(b,l)

Viv Quillin: pp. 29, 67(r)

Neath Museum, Neath Port Talbot Museum Service: p. 30(r)

Media Wales Ltd.: pp. 32, 68(t)

iStockphoto: p. 35(r), 126(b)

Solo Syndication/Associated Newspapers Ltd./National Library of Wales: pp. 35(l)(ILW02331), 67(l)(ILW01256),

Gwenda Lloyd Wallace: pp. 37(t), 66(c,r)

National Federation of Women's Institutes (NFWI): p. 37(b)

The Advertising Archives: pp. 38, 41(t)

Gomer Press: p. 39(b,l)

© Warrington Museum & Art Gallery: p. 47(t)

Imperial War Museum: pp. 49(l)(Art.IWM PST 0402), 49(b,r) (Q108454), 50(l)(Art. IWM PST 5489), 51(b,l)(IWM PST 13171), 51(b,r)(IWM PST 2766), 55(t,l)(Art. IWM PST 2832), 59(Q30038)

Gwynedd Archives Service: p. 51(t)(XS2023.6e)

Catrin Stevens: pp. 53(l), 55(b,r)

Women's Archive of Wales Collection: p. 55(b,l)

Punch Limited: pp. 57(t,r), 89(b)

Beti Isabel Hughes: p. 57(b,l)

©Roger Turvey: Roger Turvey, *Wales and Britain 1906-1951* (London: Hodder Arnold H&S, 1997), p. 139: p. 58(t)

Richard Huw Pritchard: p. 61(b,l)

Ceredigion County Council: p. 64(r)

Photoshot: p. 65(b,l)

North Wales Weekly News: p. 68(r)

Jacky Fleming: pp. 75(b), 80(b)

Souvenir Press: Elaine Morgan, *The Descent of Woman: The Classic Study of Evolution* (London: Souvenir Press, 2001): p. 76(t,r)

Aberystwyth University/Vince Jones: p. 82(c)

Laura Ashley Ltd.: p. 83(b)

Press Association: p. 96(b,r)

© National Portrait Gallery, London: p. 101(r)

HarperCollins Publishers Ltd.: © Germaine Greer, *The Female Eunuch* (London: Harper Perennial, 2006): p. 108(t,r)

Martin Shakeshaft: p. 111(b,l)

© Science Museum/Science & Society Picture Library: p. 112(l)

London Evening Standard/Solo Syndication/British Cartoon Archive: p. 120(l)

Associated Newspapers Ltd./Solo Syndication/National Library of Wales: p. 124(l)

Thank you to the following for kind permission to reproduce extracts:

Ceredigion County Council: *Annual Report of the County Medical Officer of Health FOR THE YEAR 1913* (Aberystwyth: Cardiganshire County Council, 1913), p. 33: p. 2

Hughes a'i Fab/S4C: Moelona, *Teulu Bach Nantoer* (Wrexham: Hughes a'i Fab, 1913), p. 7: p. 3

Dr Prys Morgan: Glanmor Williams (ed.), *Swansea: An Illustrated History* (Swansea: Christopher Davies Publishers Ltd., 1990), p. 210: p. 3(b)

Amgueddfa Cymru - National Museum Wales: S. Minwel Tibbott and Beth Thomas, *O'r Gwaith i'r Gwely: A Woman's Work* (Cardiff: National Museum Wales, 1994): pp. 4(c)(p. 7), 4(b)

Contents

WHAT WAS THE ROLE OF WOMEN IN THE HOME IN WALES AND ENGLAND IN THE EARLY TWENTIETH CENTURY?

Introduction

SOURCE 1

© Museum of London

A cartoon by Catherine Courtauld (1878-1972), published as a postcard in 1912

TASK

What does Source 1 tell us about attitudes towards the traditional roles of men and women at the beginning of the twentieth century?

THE TRADITIONAL ROLE OF WOMEN

During the 19th century men and women's roles were separate. Men were seen as the breadwinners, who were supposed to provide for their families by working in the public world outside the home. Women, especially wives and mothers, on the other hand, worked in the private world of the home and were expected to provide their families with comfortable, clean and well-run places to live. These worlds were considered 'separate spheres' and the ideas or 'ideology' whereby a woman's place was defined as being in the home was called **'domestic ideology'**. These traditional ideas were very influential throughout the twentieth century too.

In coal-mining, slate-quarrying and other areas of heavy industry in Wales, the working class women conformed to the notion of 'separate spheres'. In these areas an ideal picture of the 'Welsh Mam' emerged. She was portrayed as a model housewife, whose husband (and son and even lodger, sometimes) handed her his weekly wage packet unopened, thus allowing her to manage all the household finances and rule her own domain in the home. She would take care of paying the rent, buying food and clothing, light, heating and insurances and generally be expected 'to make ends meet'. In fact, this practice relieved the male breadwinner of the responsibility and hardship of coping with running a household on very small wages or, if he was unemployed, on no wage at all. Far from **empowering** women, the pressure to 'manage' weighed heavily upon their shoulders.

Working-class women as homemakers before 1914

As women spent far more time than men in the home, the standard of housing affected them far more. It was considered an essentially female issue. Many houses in rural, urban and industrial areas throughout Wales and England were in a poor condition and little more than slums. Most had no indoor toilet, running water, electricity or adequate ventilation. Overcrowding was very common due to the large size of families and the custom of taking in lodgers.

In industrial areas many families still lived in cellars with no natural light or ventilation, or in **two-up, two-down** houses. In some areas of Merthyr Tydfil, for example, there were **over and under** houses, with the under houses backing on to damp earth.

SOURCE 2

Overcrowding in a poor home, pre-1914

TASK

How far does Source 2 support the information in this section? Explain your answer.

SOURCE 3

Accommodation could be even worse in rural areas although pretty white-washed cottages might give a different impression. In Abermarchnad, Cricieth, ten dwellings shared five earth closets (toilets), had no back doors and only skylights for ventilation.

a large percentage of so-called "houses" deserve no better term than "hovels," as one often finds them with leaky roofs, floors and walls saturated with damp, wall paper peeling and mildewed, storm water flowing through living rooms, windows small and never intended to be opened and in some localities, notably so in Cwmystwyth, "back-to-earth" cottages abound.

From the Annual Report of the County Medical Officer of Health on rural housing in Cardiganshire (Ceredigion), 1913

Although small, the little cottage was remarkably cosy and safe. When the storm blew at its most violent over the barren vastness of the heath, its sturdy walls were not shaken, and the heaviest rain could barely be heard through its snug thatched roof.

From Teulu Bach Nantoer, *a children's novel by Moelona (Elizabeth Mary Jones (formerly Owen)) describing a cottage in Ceredigion c. 1913*

A typical cottage in Aberdaron on the Llŷn peninsula pre-1914

TASKS

1. Study Sources 3 and 4. Which do you consider to be the most accurate regarding working class housing in rural Wales pre-1914? Why?

2. Could they both be accurate?

3. Would you say that Source 5 illustrates Source 3 or Source 4 best?

One consequence of living in **unsanitary** and poorly built homes was the **prevalence of diseases** such as tuberculosis (TB), poliomyelitis (Polio) and rickets. 117,000 people were suffering from TB in Britain in 1913, polio crippled thousands of poor children and rickets weakened bones. In most cases it was the mother who had to cope with these diseases on the family hearth. When Megan Lloyd George became Wales' first-ever female MP in 1929, she used her **maiden speech** in the House of Commons to highlight the link between poor housing, poverty and TB.

However there was some better quality housing available for skilled industrial workers. The Lewis Merthyr Colliery Company in the Rhondda built a new village for its workers at Llwyncelyn between 1890 and 1902 and the Tredegar Iron and Coal Company began work on a village at Oakdale in 1907. These houses had a piped water supply and water closets.

In Swansea the Corporation (the town council) took advantage of the powers in the Housing and the Working Classes Act of 1890 to demolish unfit premises and build council houses. A 'garden village' was designed for the mountain top site at Townhill / Mayhill in 1912. As historian Prys Morgan said in 1990:

SOURCE 6

It is clear that in Swansea there was great public interest in workers' housing, and that strenuous efforts were made by environmental groups in conjunction with the municipality in the opening years of this century to solve the housing crisis in most imaginative ways.

Although this scheme had to be put on hold during the First World War (1914-18), by the late 1920s there were several extensive council estates in Swansea.

Council housing in Mayhill, post 1918

Household and family tasks and routines

During this period working class housewives did not go out to work to earn a wage and they were not paid for devoting themselves to their homes. In order to complete the housework expected of them they followed a strict routine. Each day would have its allocated tasks, week in week out, with no free weekends, holidays or overtime pay for an 18-hour day in many cases. It was a life sentence for women.

Every day had its work. Washing on Monday. Usually we'd iron on a Tuesday morning. And then we'd make bread. We'd bake on a Wednesday morning and make cakes. We'd do the churning on a Thursday ... and ... [the] cleaning. Cleaning the bedrooms, and the small room – the specials, you know. Of course on Friday it was the kitchen's turn. That took a day in itself. ... And then on Saturday we cleaned outside, and the yards. Friday afternoon we'd go to town with the eggs. ... And Saturday, we'd cook ready for Sunday.

*The **oral testimony** of Mrs Annie Mainwaring, Margam (born 1880). She also notes that, as she lived on a farm, this housework had to be fitted in around all the other outside work on the farm itself.*

The water was quite scarce, so we had to carry every drop of water from the river ... We'd get drinking water from the well, but water from the river was good enough for washing ... People these days don't know about anything like that. They only have to turn a tap – the water's there.

The oral testimony of Mrs Elizabeth Evans, Bethesda, Gwynedd (born 1910)

These housewives did not have the amenities and equipment we have today and housework could be very burdensome. Water had to be carried from wells or stand pipes and then heated on a coal-fire. Cleaning the grate and disposing of the ashes was a dirty job in itself. Clothes were washed in tin baths or wooden tubs, using a wash board or a dolly for heavy items. Washing dirty work clothes, whether those of farm labourers, quarrymen or coal miners was particularly challenging. In wet weather these clothes had to be dried indoors, making the atmosphere even more damp and uncomfortable. Ironing was a demanding task when the flat iron had to be heated in front of the fire.

The hardest work for the wife of a **smallholder** or quarryman was washing his working clothes. ... the slate dust went all over them, didn't it? But they were washed once a month, and that was an awful job! ... We had a saucepan to wash clothes. ... My mother – I don't know how she did it – would carry this big oval saucepan with the clothes inside it and put it under the water spout to rinse them, in all kinds of weather.

Dr Kate Roberts, a famous Welsh author, describing the tedious task of washing working men's clothes in Rhostryfan, Gwynedd pre-1914

*Mrs Agnes Lloyd, Llantrisant, washing clothes with a corrugated zinc washboard out on the **bailey** in the 1930s*

TASKS

1. Use the sources in this section and your own knowledge to compile a list of the household tasks that women had to undertake during this period.

2. Write a newspaper article highlighting the drudgery involved in such housework.

In coal mining districts another challenge faced the conscientious housewife, because the miners bathed, after a hard day at the coalface, in tin baths in front of the fire. Water had to be heated and then carried to these baths; this was heavy and dangerous work and the chances of scalding themselves and their children were ever present. Sometimes two or three colliers lived in the same house but worked different shifts, so that the tedious routine of bathing, with all its dangers and dirt, had to be repeated several times a day. Typically, the wife would wash her husband's back, in spite of the generally held belief that washing weakened the spinal chord. Yet, in spite of these challenges many working class housewives found housework fulfilling and were very proud of their spotlessly clean homes and families. 'We were poor but we were clean' was the oft-repeated remark and to be considered a 'tidy woman' (*decha* in Welsh) was the highest accolade. They competed to be the first to hang out a clean line of washing and even scrubbed the pavement outside their front doors on their hands and knees in their canvas aprons. Indeed, when the Pilgrims' Trust (an American charity) conducted a sample study of 76 families in the Rhondda in 1934, 86% of the houses were described as clean and 88% of home management was described as 'good', although many of the families were unemployed and poor.

Dick is a popular man with my mother on weekends. ... On weekends, as my father says, "Dick will beat hell out of your mother's coconut mats." On Saturdays ... Dick scrubs the floor, black leads the grate and shines the brass – but he leaves the brass knocker and the front steps to me, not to show the world that he is doing a woman's work.

Barbara Walters of Glyncorrwg, near Port Talbot, describing her uncle, who lodged with her mining family in the early 1930s

In her book *Out of the Shadows: A History of Women in Twentieth-Century Wales,* (2000), the feminist historian Deirdre Beddoe comments:

SOURCE 13

Unlike coal or slate, we do not have the tonnage figures for sheets washed, dried and ironed, for potatoes peeled and boiled, or loaves of bread kneaded and baked in fire-side ovens. Women's work has passed unrecorded and, because it was unpaid, has not been technically recognized as work at all.

TASKS

1. How does Source 12 reflect the doctrines of 'domestic ideology' and 'separate spheres'?
2. Comment upon historian Deirdre Beddoe's interpretation of the value of women's work in the home in Source 13.

WOMEN IN UPPER-CLASS HOUSEHOLDS

There were other important divisions within society in the early twentieth century. These were class divisions, broadly between the upper, the middle and the working classes and these divisions affected women as much as they did men. The notion of 'separate spheres' was also as relevant to upper-class women as it was to those of the working classes.

Edwardian 'High Society'

Although Edward VII was only king from 1902 to 1910, the whole of the period between the turn of the century and the First World War is regarded as the Edwardian Age. This was an era when the established **landed gentry** and the newly rich, who had made their fortunes through trade, business and industry, owned vast estates and large mansions and lived lives of luxury and indulgence. Many owned several mansions and would change houses according to the 'season', visiting their country houses in Wales, for example, only for the hunting and shooting season in the autumn. The Pennant family, who owned Penrhyn Castle near Bangor and the huge Penrhyn slate quarries, also had estates in Northamptonshire, as well as a house in Belgravia, a wealthy area of London.

In their stately homes the upper classes entertained lavishly. A modest dinner party would have included at least eight courses. When the feasting was over the women would leave the main dining room to be served their coffee separately, while the men smoked and drank some more. It is little wonder that this period became known as *La Belle Epoque* (the beautiful era).

SOURCE 14

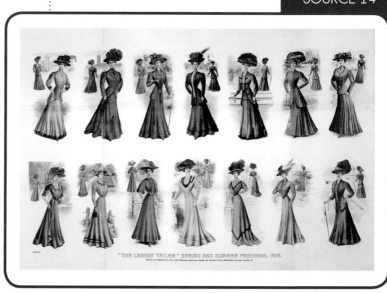

Edwardian fashion plate for Ladies' spring and summer fashions, 1909

Many Edwardian ladies took part in countryside sports and also enjoyed playing tennis, watching horse racing at Ascot and the Derby, and sailing at Cowes on the Isle of Wight. They also participated enthusiastically in the new sports of bicycling and driving a motor car. For all these social occasions they would be expected to dress appropriately in the latest London fashions.

An Edwardian lady was also expected to hand out charity amongst the working classes and the poor within her sphere of influence. This emphasised her superior position within society.

If Mrs Heneage passed, the schoolchildren always had to curtsy. ...

At Christmas time we had big Sunday School parties in the great hall at Coker Court. The people who were not so well off, the Heneages used to buy shoes or boots for the children

The reminiscences of residents of East Coker, near Yeovil, Somerset, c. 1910 about the Heneage family (relatives of the Vivians of Swansea) who lived in the mansion at Coker Court

TASKS

1. Discuss the advantages of being an Edwardian lady pre-1914, using Sources 14-15 and the other information provided here.

2. Write two sentences each to reflect the attitudes of Mrs Heneage on the one hand and those who received her charity on the other in Source 15.

'Upstairs, Downstairs'

To help keep up their way of life the upper classes employed a range of servants. These would have included male gardeners and estate workers as well as several house-servants. Once more the doctrine of 'separate spheres' ruled in a stately home, where the roles of male and female servants were clearly defined and unassailable (could not be changed).

At the head of the household would be the main male member of the landed gentry family. He would be responsible for the finances of the estate and mansion and for hiring the staff. The senior lady of the house would be in charge of the household staff and oversaw the day-to-day running of the house. Her role was to give orders from 'Upstairs' to those who worked 'Downstairs'. She did not do any of the housework herself; for example Lady Penrhyn of Penrhyn Castle, near Bangor, would meet the housekeeper every morning to decide upon the daily duties. Penrhyn employed a modest number of servants at this time: 41 (23 of whom were female); compared with Kinmel Park, near Abergele, Conwy with its 68 indoor servants. The **census returns** for 1901 and 1911 provide useful information about the staff employed in these great houses and their respective roles.

The family and servants of Erddig Hall, near Wrexham, in 1912. In the window 'Upstairs' are Phillip Yorke II and his wife, Louise Matilda and their two children. Among the 'Downstairs' staff we see: back row – Lucy Hitchman, Head Nurse (carrying children's shoes to symbolise her work); Alice Jones, Head Laundress (linen); Mary Ellis, Second Laundry Maid (linen); Edith Haycock, Housemaid (brush); front row – Rose Williams, Cook (pigeon); Miss Brown, Housekeeper (keys) and Bessie Gittins, Under Housemaid (brush)

The Housekeeper supervised all the maidservants, except the **lady's maid**, the nurse and the cook; she looked after the household accounts and bought in supplies and looked after their storage. She would have her own headquaters within the house. Under the housekeeper came a whole **hierarchy** of maids, including housemaids, laundry, dairy and **still room** maids, and at the bottom would be the hapless scullery maid who had to clean and light the kitchen range and do mountains of washing-up. These maids slept in attic rooms with inadequate lighting, heating and washing facilities.

SOURCE 17

There are 22 servants in the house ... there are five in the Kitchen + two regularly in the scullery. I am afraid Miss Brown that sounds very much like a fairy tale, but, when I tell you there are fourteen cold meats sent up every day for my Lord's Luncheon ... you will understand there is some work to be done in the Kitchen alone. Then my Lord has a clean table cloth for every meal. Is it not ridiculous? ... I often say if cleanliness would keep any one alive, then Viscount Tredegar would never die.

A letter written by one of the servants at Tredegar House, near Newport, to the housekeeper at Erddig Hall, Wrexham, 5 March 1911

SOURCE 18

1901 CENSUS. HUNTINGDON ST MARY'S			HINCHINGBROOKE HOUSE		
Name	*Reln to H*	*Cond*	*Age*	*Occupation*	*Where Born*
Harry Hill	Servant	Un	20	Odd Man	Hunts Brampton
Henry Cooper	Head	Un	56	House Steward	Hunts Brampton
Elizabeth Howe	Servant	Un	40	Housekeeper	Dorset Piddleton
Harriet Jordan	Servant	Un	27	Laundry Maid	Staffords Elmhurst
Florence Putner	Servant	Un	19	Laundry Maid	Middlesex Lambeth
Charlotte Gilbert	Servant	Un	29	Stillroom Maid	Northants Burghley
Ann Clough	Servant	Un	53	Dairy Maid	Yorks Hornbey
Sarah Ann Taylor	Servant	Un	26	Kitchen Maid	Hants Ramsey St Mary's
Louisa Smith	Servant	Un	19	Scullery Maid	Rutlandshire Kelton
Elizabeth Wass	Servant	Un	27	House Maid	Notts Norwell
Lilly Hagram	Servant	Un	21	House Maid	Middlesex Bayswater
Mary Usher	Servant	Un	19	House Maid	Hunts Buckden
John Lissenden	Servant	Un	32	Under Butler	Kent Malling
George .. Gregor	Servant	Un	28	Footman	Scotland
George Andrews	Servant	Un	23	Footman	Somerset Shepton Mallet
Charles Ernest Dale	Servant	Un	26	Footman	Oxfordshire Addebury

Key:
Reln to H – relationship to Head of Household; *Cond* – Condition; *Un* – Unmarried

A list of servants at Hinchingbrooke House, Huntingdon, Cambridgeshire, 1901

TASKS

1. What do Sources 16 and 17 tell us about the nature of the relationship between servants and their masters?

2. Compare and contrast the number of servants at Erddig Hall in 1912 and at Hinchinbrooke House in 1901. Why are the Master and Mistress of Hinchingbrooke not recorded on the census form?

3. Conduct your own research from the Census Returns for 1901 or 1911 on a stately home in your area.

The Middle Classes

Between the upper and working class households, there were the households of the middle classes. Many middle class people owned their own homes often on estates in the suburbs of towns and cities. These houses were built in pairs and had bay-windows and three upstairs bedrooms. Professional people, such as solicitors, doctors, teachers, farmers and tradesmen were members of the middle classes. These households also kept one or two maid-servants to do all the menial household tasks. *Mrs Beeton's Book of Household Management*, a best-seller for many decades after it was first published in 1861, was regarded as the foolproof guide to the management of such a household. It gave advice on its organization, the management of servants and **modern housecraft.**

WOMEN IN THE 1930s

After the First World War the soldiers returned home to a promise of 'a Land fit for Heroes' where there would be 'Homes fit for Heroes', based upon the aims of the Addison Housing Act of 1919.

Unfortunately such optimism soon evaporated as the traditional heavy industries of coal, steel, shipbuilding, textiles and slate went into serious decline. This affected the north of England and the industrial regions of Wales in particular. There was little relief in rural areas either as agriculture faced a very lean period too. The General Strike of 1926 and the Wall Street Crash in the USA in 1929 made the situation worse for the working classes. This led to the Great Depression of the 1930s with mass unemployment undermining the traditional way of life in many parts of Britain. In 1933, 18.6% of the workers in England were unemployed. In Wales the figure was 35.4%, with Breconshire topping the charts at 51.9%, Anglesey second at 40.8%, Monmouthshire at 42% and Glamorganshire at 40.4%. As a result around 400,000 people emigrated from Wales in search of work.

The role of women in the depressed areas

The long economic depression had a devastating effect upon the lives of women as they struggled to 'make ends meet' with very little resources. The effect that this had, especially on women's health and well-being, was terrible as they 'went without' in order to feed their families. Studies in the 1930s showed that many suffered from debilitating (weakening) illnesses. Often women grew old before their time.

SOURCE 19

The children are hungry, the men are hungry; but most hungry of all are the women who deprive themselves so that their husbands and their children can eat a little more. ...
While the unemployed man succumbs to idleness, his wife deteriorates from overwork.

American Eli Ginzberg's observations on the situation in south-east Wales in the 1930s in A World Without Work: The Story of the Welsh Miners

SOURCE 20

An attempt is being made ... by certain members of Parliament and ... the Press, to attribute the widespread malnutrition ... to ignorance, obstinacy, and laziness on the part of the housewives and mothers of families, rather than to the true cause, which is lack of sufficient funds to purchase any of the expensive "protective" foods such as milk and vegetables.

Dame Juliet Rhys-Williams of Miskin Manor, near Caerffili, addressing the Welsh School of Social Science at Llandrindod Wells in 1936

Mrs E. M. W. of Pontypool, Monmouth. There are nine in the family, the ages of the children being fourteen, thirteen, eleven, seven, five, three, and two. The income from all sources is £2 7s. [£2.35] a week. ... the family has only one kettle, one small frying-pan, two small saucepans. ... seven cups and saucers between nine ... The house is old and very damp and cold. ... The mother is now suffering from a skin disease ... brought on by poor quality food and nervous tension.

An extract from The Problem of the Distressed Areas *by Wal Hannington, 1937*

as it was Thursday – the day we used to call starvation day – we had nothing in the house. No food and no money. ...

At this time men were getting very depressed and frustrated. ... So whatever went wrong ... they would take it out on their wives and children. You often saw a woman with bruises or a black eye walking about.

The oral testimony of Beatrice Wood, born in Dowlais in 1916

TASK

What do the sources in this section tell us about how working class women 'managed' during the Great Depression?

The Means Test

This depressing situation was made worse by the hated Means Test, introduced by the new National (Coalition) Government in 1931. An unemployed man had been able to claim benefit (called the dole) for the first six months of unemployment. But now he had to prove that he needed the dole – it was means tested for the first time. All the family's income would be taken into account. If a son or daughter living at home was in employment, the benefit would be reduced accordingly. It was felt that this was an intrusion into private family affairs.

With unemployment soaring, the government introduced a further measure – the Unemployment Insurance Act of 1934. This set up the Unemployment Assistance Boards (UABs), which sought to ensure that only those 'desperately in need' received benefits and then only if they were 'actively seeking work'. This was an insult to people in areas where there was no work available or where sickness prevented them from working.

In spite of the hardship and poverty that came in the wake of these new measures we must be careful not to depict women as mere helpless victims of their circumstances. In fact, they often responded to these challenges with determination and courage. They organized Relief Centres to distribute second hand clothing and shoes and soup kitchens to feed the hungry.

The ship-building areas of north-east England suffered extreme hardship due to unemployment and poverty in the 1930s too. This sculpture, called the 'Spirit of Jarrow', was erected in 2001 to commemorate the Jarrow Crusade march to London to highlight unemployment in 1936. In the front walks Ellen Wilkinson (Red Ellen), M.P. for Jarrow

Welsh women joined in the protests against the government. When a Hunger March left south Wales in 1934, twelve women in bright red berets led the way. When the UABs came into operation in February 1935, the women joined in the mass protests in the valleys. Then an army of angry women, led by Ceridwen Brown of Aberdare, broke into the UAB's offices in Merthyr Tydfil and wrecked them. The next day the government put the new scales of benefit on hold.

SOURCE 24

Well you couldn't not take part in any activity which would make people themselves feel that at least they were fighting back and also you felt it was absolutely essential to get other people to understand the enormity of the situation.

Oral testimony of Dora Cox, one of the hunger marchers (Source 25) on their way to London from south Wales in 1934

SOURCE 25

Hunger marchers on the outskirts of Slough, 23 February 1934, on their way from south Wales to London

Another way in which the women tried to take control of their own lives was by campaigning for **pithead baths**, to eliminate the dirt and dangers of miners bathing in their own homes. The Ocean Coal Company of Treharris (due to the influence of the owner's sisters, the Misses Davies of Llandinam) opened baths in 1916, but others were slow to follow suit. One of the leading campaigners was Elizabeth Andrews.

SOURCE 26

- Born in Hirwaun in the Cynon Valley to a mining family, she left school at twelve to help at home.
- She appeared on behalf of the South Wales Miners Federation before the Sankey Commission in 1919, to argue for pithead baths. Yet she says:

  "... amongst the miners and their families, prejudices had to be overcome, old ideas destroyed and convincing facts marshalled to prove the benefit of pit baths."

  (From *A Woman's Work is Never Done*, page 27)
- She worked as the first woman organizer for the Labour Party in Wales.
- Her autobiography *A Woman's Work is Never Done* was published in 1957.
- Favourite motto: Educate, agitate, organize!

Elizabeth Andrews (1882-1960)

The Depression, however, did not have the same devastating affect on every part of Britain. In England, parts of the Midlands, London and the south-east, prospered, thanks mainly to the success of light industry and the manufacturing of cars. In Wales, Flintshire was relatively prosperous with its new rayon manufacturing, steel works and building industries. Tourism enabled seaside towns, such as Rhyl, Prestatyn and Llandudno in north Wales and Porthcawl and Tenby in the south to flourish. The anthracite coalfield and the tinplate industry in south-west Wales escaped the worst of the Depression. Cardiff, Neath, Wrexham, Llanelli and Swansea developed substantially. During the 1930s the use of electricity was widespread in Swansea and a new main drainage scheme was introduced to improve sanitation. The Corporation provided 2,399 new homes between 1931 and 1939 and 2,000 new private houses were built for the middle classes, mainly in the Sketty area. In these homes mass-produced goods, such as the electric vacuum cleaner and cookers, began to appear.

Even in the depressed areas, people found light relief by escaping to the world of Hollywood in the ever popular cinemas and jazz bands, male voice choirs and carnivals also provided plenty of entertainment. Under the Special Area scheme, the Council for Social Services set up Women's Clubs to run needlework and craft courses and drama societies were formed. By 1939 there were 260 such clubs in south Wales.

As historian David Egan points out:

SOURCE 27

It would be wrong to suggest that everything ... was depressed or depressing. There was still plenty of vitality and fight in the people and communities of the coalfield.

TASKS

1. Study the sources in this section. Discuss how women tried to overcome the difficulties that faced them in the 1930s. Were women fundamentally challenging their role as home-makers?

2. Research the Jarrow Crusade to find out more about MP Ellen Wilkinson and why she was called 'Red Ellen'.

Examination practice

This section provides guidance on how to answer question 1(b) from Units 1 and 2. It is a source comprehension question, which is linked to the recall of your own factual knowledge and is worth 4 marks.

Question 1(b) – comprehension of a source and the recall of own knowledge

Use the information in Source A and your own knowledge to explain why the 1930s were difficult for women.

[4 marks]

SOURCE A

But it was not easy to find money for the glass of cider or the package of cigarettes that they knew would help, and many were the deprivations that the women inflicted on themselves so that their husbands might not become utterly miserable.

American Eli Ginzberg in A World Without Work: The Story of the Welsh Miners, *following a visit to south-east Wales during the 1930s*

Tips on how to answer

- Read through the source, **underlining or highlighting** the key points.

- In your answer you should **try and rephrase and explain these points** in your own words.

- Aim to bring in your **own background knowledge** to expand upon these points.

- Think about any **other relevant factors** that are not included in the source and bring them into your answer.

- To obtain maximum marks **you need to do two things**: refer to information from **the source** and add to this information from your **own knowledge** of this topic area.

Response by candidate one

Women found it difficult to buy cider and cigarettes for their husbands. Sometimes they went without things to please their husbands who were out of work. All this meant that life was difficult in the home for them because they had to try to keep everybody happy during difficult times.

> Paraphrases the source

> Some credit for the last sentence

Examiner's comment

This answer lacks any real development. The candidate has paraphrased the content of the source only. There is no attempt to place the source into its historical context. The candidate has not used any additional knowledge. The final sentence does make reference to the difficulties of women. This answer would only achieve 1 mark for one observation.

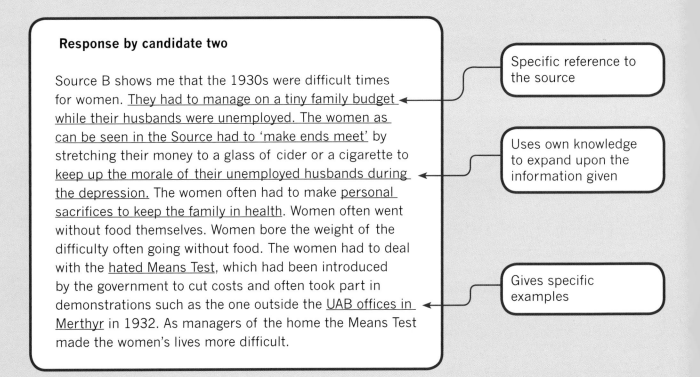

Response by candidate two

Source B shows me that the 1930s were difficult times for women. <u>They had to manage on a tiny family budget while their husbands were unemployed. The women as can be seen in the Source had to 'make ends meet'</u> by stretching their money to a glass of cider or a cigarette to <u>keep up the morale of their unemployed husbands during the depression.</u> The women often had to make <u>personal sacrifices to keep the family in health</u>. Women often went without food themselves. Women bore the weight of the difficulty often going without food. The women had to deal with the <u>hated Means Test</u>, which had been introduced by the government to cut costs and often took part in demonstrations such as the one outside the <u>UAB offices in Merthyr</u> in 1932. As managers of the home the Means Test made the women's lives more difficult.

Specific reference to the source

Uses own knowledge to expand upon the information given

Gives specific examples

Examiner's comment

This is a well developed answer. The candidate has demonstrated a sound understanding of the topic and has worked the source material well. The candidate has introduced some background knowledge and context and expands upon the information given in the source. The response is worthy of 4 marks.

Now you have a go

SOURCE B

The overriding theme here is ... constraint and sacrifice. ...
   While the miners were working a seven-hour day ... their wives' working day was nearer seventeen, perhaps even longer, depending on the requirement to get up to make breakfast for husbands, sons or lodgers on the early shift. ... It can be said that the women's work in their homes was as well regulated and as rigidly structured as the men's

Carol White and Sian Rhiannon Williams in their introduction to Struggle or Starve: Stories of everyday heroism between the wars *(2009)*

Question

Use the information in Source B and your own knowledge to explain why life was difficult for women in the depressed areas like south Wales.

[4 marks]

CHAPTER 2

HOW DID LIFE FOR WOMEN AT HOME IN WALES AND ENGLAND CHANGE AFTER THE SECOND WORLD WAR?

Introduction

SOURCE 1

At the beginning of this century [20th], the expectation of life of a woman aged twenty was forty-six years.[2] Approximately one-third of this ... was to be devoted to ... childbearing and maternal care in infancy. Today [1963], the expectation of life of a woman aged twenty is fifty-five years. Of this ... only about 7 per cent of the years to be lived will be concerned with childbearing and maternal care in infancy.

[2] English Life Table, No. 7 for 1901-10, Supplement to the 75th Annual Report of the Registrar-General, Pt 1, 1914.

Richard M. Titmuss in Essays on 'The Welfare State', 1963

TASK

What does Source 1 suggest about improvements in women's health between 1900 and 1958?

THE EFFECTS OF GOVERNMENT LEGISLATION

Background

Even during the Second World War the Coalition Government was planning for a better Britain, when peace would be eventually declared. It was particularly anxious to avoid any repetition of the great depression of the 1930s. Since the beginning of the twentieth century the state had been intervening in people's lives to try to improve their lot, through such measures as Old Age Pensions (1906), the National Insurance Act (1911) and other reforms. The **reconstruction programme** of the 1940s developed these reforms further.

The reconstruction programme was based upon the report *Social Insurance and Allied Services* by William Beveridge, which appeared in 1942. It identified the problem of the 'Five Evil Giants': Want (poverty), Ignorance, Disease, Idleness and Squalor (dirt) and suggested how these problems could be tackled by a post-war government. It aimed at caring for the people 'from the cradle to the grave' by providing:

- A comprehensive health system;
- Vastly expanded public housing;
- Free and universal secondary education;
- Full employment;
- Benefits for the poor;
- Family allowances.

This programme would be paid for through flat rate compulsory contributions payable through income tax and national insurance.

As far as women were concerned there was a great deal in the report that would benefit their lives immensely. However, there were also serious weaknesses in it. The report stressed the importance of the family as an economic unit. In fact, it was based on the principle that women would take on their traditional pre-war 'normal' roles as full-time wives and mothers after the war. It promoted the notion that men and women were 'equal but different' and that they had distinctive roles to play in society.

TACKLING THE FIRST GIANT

"WANT is only one of the five giants on the road of reconstruction." — The Beveridge Report.

A cartoon of William Beveridge attacking the problems of the 'Five Evil Giants' of post Second World War Britain, December 1942

Taken as a whole, the Plan for Social Security puts a premium on [rewards] marriage, in place of penalising it ... In the next thirty years housewives as mothers have vital work to do in ensuring the adequate continuance of the British race and of British ideals in the world.

From the Beveridge Report of 1942 (p.52-53, par.117)

TASKS

1. Consider how the six points proposed in the Beveridge Report (noted above) would help to tackle the five evil giants shown in the cartoon in Source 2.

2. Using Source 3, explain the role that women were expected to play in the reconstruction of Britain, according to the Beveridge Report.

However, in general, the Beveridge Report was immensely popular and became a best-seller. When the Labour Party won a landslide victory in the general election in 1945, it was determined to implement its main proposals. This led to the establishment of the Welfare State (1945-50). The Welfare State was a term used to describe the cluster of welfare reforms passed through government legislation at this time. The first important step to building the Welfare State had already been passed in 1944, when the Butler Education Act provided free secondary education for all, up to the compulsory age of 15 (with provision for raising it to 16). This Act transformed the educational opportunities open to girls and the working classes in particular.

Family allowances

In 1945 the Family Allowances Act, which provided child benefit for the first time in Britain, was passed by parliament. However, women had been campaigning for this reform for thirty years, especially once they had won the right to vote in 1918 and 1928. One tireless campaigner was Eleanor Rathbone (1872-1946), who, with other members of the Family Endowment Society in 1917, published a pamphlet called *Equal Pay and the Family. A Proposal for the National Endowment of Motherhood.* She saw motherhood as a service to the community – a service that should be acknowledged though regular payments by the state.

In 1929 Rathbone became an MP and continued her campaigning in parliament and through another persuasive pamphlet entitled *A Case for Family Allowances*. It is interesting to compare her demands and the actual terms of the Act of 1945 (see Source 4). Some trade unions were opposed to family allowances because they were afraid that employers would pay lower wages because of them. Ironically, Eleanor Rathbone died before the act was implemented for the first time in 1946. Before she died however, she was able to influence the government to change its policy, and to pay the allowance directly to mothers rather than to fathers within the family unit. In 1946 family allowances were paid out to 2.5 million families. Child Benefit replaced Family Allowances in 1975.

SOURCE 4

Proposals for Family Allowances, 1917 (Rathbone and others)	Family Allowances Act, 1945
Weekly payments of: – 2s.6d (63p) to the wife – 5s (25p) for the first child – 3s 6d for every other child	Weekly payments of: 5s for every second child and every subsequent child in the family

SOURCE 5

Eleanor Rathbone, who was featured on a 'Women of Achievement' stamp in 2008

SOURCE 6

A mother in Stratford collecting her first Family Allowance payment on 6 August 1946

TASKS

1. Study Source 4. Compare the proposals for family allowances in 1917 and the actual terms of the 1945 Act.

2. Why was Eleanor Rathbone (Source 5) chosen as one of the six women to be commemorated on the 'Women of Achievement' stamps in 2008?

3. Write a short newspaper article to go with the picture in Source 6 and from your own knowledge of the subject.

National Insurance

The National Health Insurance Act of 1911, passed when Welshman, David Lloyd George, was Chancellor of the Exchequer, gave the British working class its first **contributory system of insurance** against illness and unemployment. The Act also provided a lump sum maternity payment of 30s (£1.50) to the wives of insured workers when a baby was born. At first, the government intended paying this sum to the father of the family, but the Women's Co-operative Guild campaigned vigorously to ensure that it would be paid directly to the mother. One important flaw in the 1911 Act was that it made no provision for sickness payments for the wives of the contributors – they would not benefit from the Act.

In the post-Second World War period it was obvious that a new Insurance Act was required. James Griffiths, MP for Llanelli, became the Minister for National Insurance and was charged with the task of delivering it. Under the terms of the Act passed in 1946, employees and employers would make compulsory contributions towards unemployment, sickness, maternity and widows' benefits, as well as old age pensions and funeral grants, with the government funding the balance. It was, according to James Griffiths 'the best and cheapest insurance offered to the British people of any people anywhere.' Once again, however, because married women didn't pay national insurance contributions they could not claim benefits in their own right. They were still in an inferior position and remained dependent upon their husband. Even married women who worked were not expected to make National Insurance contributions and could not claim benefits in their own right. A single working woman paid a lower national insurance contribution than a man because, it was argued, she did not have a family to support.

The National Health Service (NHS)

Background

The most controversial piece of government legislation passed by the post-war Labour government was the National Health Service Act of 1946. Yet, no one could doubt that the health system needed a complete overhaul in post-war Wales and England. Before this, many hospitals were being run by charities or local authorities and there was no uniform system of care. Dental operations were often carried out on kitchen tables and the usual remedy for whooping cough was to stand the patient near a steam roller tarring the road. Most of the working classes could not afford to pay for consultations with doctors; others ran up debts in private hospitals. Many sick and elderly people had to enter the workhouse or remain untreated.

Women, in particular, tended to suffer silently in ill health. In 1933, the Women's Health Enquiry Committee launched an investigation into married women's health. The committee's findings were published in *Working Class Wives: Their Health and Condition* by Margery Spring Rice in 1939. 1,250 women responded to the enquiry's questionnaire and the conclusions confirmed the suspicion that working class women were worn down by poor housing, large families and poor diet.

SOURCE 7

Mrs. F. of Sheffield. She is 47 and has had seven children, of whom two have died. Her husband is a railway drayman. She gets £2 17s. 0d. [£2.85] housekeeping ... She has rheumatism, ... toothache, headache and back-ache. For none of these does she consult anyone. She owes her private doctor for the last five years' attendance, including the last confinement [birth], £14, which she pays off in 1/– [5p] weekly instalments

Margery Spring Rice, Working Class Wives: Their Health and Condition (1981)

SOURCE 8

A woman in Leeds who has had nine children of whom the seventh and eighth have died, has 44/– a week housekeeping money, and a poor house; she suffers from anaemia, neurasthenia and loss of appetite. She has a private doctor who "advises rest, nourishment and not to worry". ... Another [mother] in London with six children says "My Doctor before each child advised always rest and usually bed which is practically impossible."

Margery Spring Rice, Working Class Wives: Their Health and Condition *(1981)*

·NEVER·MOTHER'S·TURN·

Cartoon 'Never Mother's Turn', 1920s

The report concluded that women believed that they 'mustn't grumble' about their situation or their condition. They showed a general disinclination to fuss about themselves, which was the result of their exhausting work, their preoccupation with the welfare of their families and ignorance. Some women simply failed to apply to themselves what they did know about health in general. Advice wasn't sought as often as it should be or if sought, wasn't taken.

TASKS

1. Using Sources 7 and 8 explain why married women tended to 'suffer silently' in the pre-war period.

2. Does Source 9 support this view?

One very troubling issue regarding women's health in pre-war Wales and England was the high rate of **maternal mortality**. The 1918 Maternity and Child Welfare Act had tried to address this issue by encouraging local authorities to set up maternity and ante-natal clinics. Since this was not a compulsory requirement, it was tireless campaigning by local volunteers, such as Rose Davies in Aberdare and Lady Violet Mond in Swansea that secured the opening of clinics in these areas. In Wales the clinics were distributed unevenly; by 1924 there were only 8 clinics,

all in south Wales. By 1934, this number had risen to 87: 78 in the south-east; six in Flintshire, two in Denbighshire and one in Carmarthenshire.

Rather unexpectedly, this act did little to improve the maternal mortality rate. Indeed the numbers increased. During this time a death rate of over five per thousand births was regarded as extremely serious. The figures for Welsh counties were among the highest in Wales and England.

Anglesey	6.79	Denbigh	6.56	Ceredigion	6.39
Carmarthenshire	6.34	Glamorganshire	5.85	Pembrokeshire	5.70
Flintshire	5.63	Monmouthshire	5.18		

Compared with, for example:

Lancashire	5.41	West Riding/Yorkshire	5.37	Cumberland	5.20

Table: Maternal Mortality Rates per 1000 births, 1924-33

Furthermore, during the worst years of the depression, there were pockets of even higher rates in Wales. In 1934, the rate for the Rhondda was 11.99 (it had been 7.2 in 1933), and in Cwm Ogwr it was 10.7. This situation was scandalous and led to a 'save the mothers' campaign. Dame Juliet Rhys Williams of Miskin Manor, Llantrisant, believed that poverty and poor nutrition were partly responsible for the situation and, through the National Birthday Trust, she organized nourishing food parcels for pregnant mothers in the Rhondda. The results were staggering – the maternal mortality rate fell to 4.77 per 1000 births in 1935. The scheme was extended to other areas in south-east Wales but attempts to convince the Ministry of Health to extend it further to north-east England failed.

During the Second World War pregnant mothers received special attention due to a national milk scheme, which meant that they were entitled to free milk; free orange juice and cod liver oil was also supplied to them and their new babies. In the 1940s the introduction of the drug penicillin reduced the maternal mortality rate very significantly.

SOURCE 11

the mothers in Wales are suffering more than anyone else the consequences of the terrible impoverishment of the last 10 years, which reveals itself in this problem of maternal mortality. ... I have often told the miners and the people among whom I have spent my life in South Wales: "There is only one occupation that is more dangerous than yours, and that is the occupation of being a mother."

James Griffiths MP for Llanelli (Hansard, HC Deb 18 June 1937 vol 325, 755-6)

TASK

Would you say that James Griffiths' comments (Source 11) are supported by the statistics in Source 10?

The National Health Service Act, 1946

The National Health Service Act of 1946 tried to address one of Beveridge's 'Evil Giants' – Disease (see p.16), by bringing the services of hospitals, doctors, nurses, pharmacists, opticians and dentists all together under one **umbrella organization**, which would be free for all at the point of delivery. This service would not be a charity. It would be paid for by all tax-payers through income tax contributions. Aneurin Bevan, the MP for Ebbw Vale, was the Minister of Health expected to deliver this complex programme of reforms on behalf of the Labour government. He had been brought up in a mining family in Tredegar and had witnessed at first hand the suffering and ill-health that came in the wake of the great depression of the 1930s.

However, Bevan had to face bitter opposition to his ambitious plan from both the opposition party, the Conservatives, on the grounds of cost, and from the British Medical Association. Only 4,000 doctors out of the 45,000, surveyed in 1948, supported the scheme. They argued that they did not want to become civil servants, paid by the state, and they did not want to give up their private practices and lose their independence. Eventually, a compromise was reached and the National Health Services Act came into being on the 'Appointed Day', 5 July 1948.

SOURCE 12

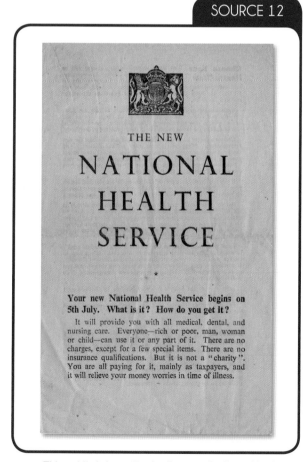

THE NEW

NATIONAL HEALTH SERVICE

Your new National Health Service begins on 5th July. What is it? How do you get it?

It will provide you with all medical, dental, and nursing care. Everyone—rich or poor, man, woman or child—can use it or any part of it. There are no charges, except for a few special items. There are no insurance qualifications. But it is not a "charity". You are all paying for it, mainly as taxpayers, and it will relieve your money worries in time of illness.

This public information leaflet was distributed by the Central Office of Information in 1948

Aneurin Bevan with the staff at the first hospital in the world to offer free healthcare to all – Park Hospital (today Trafford General), Manchester, on the day the National Health Service came into being, 5 July 1948

The NHS, for the first time ever, provided decent healthcare for all, and at a stroke transformed the lives of millions. 1,143 voluntary hospitals and 1,545 municipal hospitals were taken over in Wales and England. In Wales, the new services were put under the control of the Welsh Board of Health. There were no extra doctors or nurses. What changed was the way in which people could get and pay for care. Now people didn't pay for medical attention when they needed it; instead they paid for it collectively as taxpayers. 'From now on the "family doctor" was a person whose advice could be sought freely without incurring the previously dreaded expense', explained a Ministry of Health Report in 1949. Indeed, by then 8.5 million people had received free dental treatment and 187 million prescriptions had been dispensed. In Wales alone, by June 1954, out of a population of 2.5 million, 1.8 million pairs of free NHS spectacles had been distributed. Polio and diphtheria vaccination programmes were introduced and mass radiography campaigns for TB were extended. Other health improvements resulted from the availability of new drugs, particularly antibiotics like penicillin, 'the wonder drug' and streptomycin.

Women were particularly affected by these innovations:

SOURCE 14

at last, women had the same right to free health care as men. The extent of women's ill health became evident as much untreated chronic illness came to light. ... For Welsh women, who had been prepared to soldier on despite ill health, the service was a godsend and they took advantage of it.

Historian, Deirdre Beddoe, in Out of the Shadows, *2000*

However, it became obvious almost immediately that funding was inadequate. For example, the 2 million pounds put aside to pay for free spectacles over the first nine months had been used up within the first six weeks. This is why the Labour government was forced to introduce prescription charges of 1 shilling (5p) and a fee for dental treatment and these came into effect in 1952. As this was against the principles of the original NHS Act, Aneurin Bevan resigned from the government.

TASKS

1. What was Aneurin Bevan's contribution to the National Health Services Act? Use information from this section, Source 13 and your own knowledge to explain your answer.

2. Use the sources in this section to explain why women welcomed the NHS Act.

Many problems regarding the actual working of the NHS remain unresolved, but it can truly claim to have been a landmark social reform, for women in particular. Women are four times more likely than men to visit a doctor's surgery and they are the main recipients of prescriptions. By 2006-08 the overall maternal mortality rate had fallen to 11.39 per 100,000 births and by 2012, the life expectation for a woman had increased to 82.6 (for men to 78.4). The NHS has also introduced **preventative health measures**, e.g. campaigns for breast cancer screening, awareness of alcohol abuse and the health dangers of smoking and obesity.

FAMILY PLANNING AND PATTERNS

Birth control

In 1900 there was no reliable method of contraception and large families of up to ten children were fairly common. This meant that many mothers spent at least twenty years pregnant and caring for young children. The problem of unwanted pregnancies and having too many mouths to feed was a serious one for women. In 1915, Dr Marie Stopes (1880-1958), published *Married Love*, a book that discussed sex within marriage and recommended methods of birth control. It became an instant best-seller and thousands of desperately unhappy married women wrote to her for advice.

SOURCE 15

Please could you give me some advice about preventing my self from becoming pregnant again ... I have gone and tried to end my life ... it sends me out of my mind with the pain.

Correspondent from Norfolk to Dr Stopes, birth control campaigner, 1923

As a result, Stopes opened the first birth control clinic in Holloway, north London in 1921. Her slogan was 'Babies in the right places'. Other pioneers joined in the campaign. Dora Russell and educationalist Mary Stocks, established the Workers' Birth Control Group in 1924. A year later the first hospital birth control clinic, run by local pioneer, nurse Joyce Daniel, was opened in Abertillery, but, due to strong opposition from the local chapels, it closed in 1926. In 1929-30 Marie Stopes's caravan clinic toured south Wales and a clinic opened in Pontypridd.

The campaign gained momentum in the early 1930s with the founding of the National Birth Control Association. By now, local authorities were permitted to provide information about birth control to married women, if a pregnancy was deemed detrimental to their health. Yet, by 1937, fewer than 25% of local authorities had established such clinics. In Wales there were only 14 in 1939, mostly in the south-east. They were not very successful because they did not target working class mothers or advertise their services adequately. In the same year the Family Planning Association, with its slogan, 'Children by Choice not Chance', was founded.

SOURCE 16

(i) We want better reasons for having children than not knowing how to prevent them

(ii) even if we lived in Buckingham Palace, we would not want a baby every year.

(i) Dora Russell, birth control campaigner, 1925, in Hypatia

(ii) Dora Russell in The Tamarisk Tree, *1977*

After the war, the need for birth control advice for married women was generally accepted, although the Church of England did not finally give its blessing until 1958 and the Roman Catholic Church remained opposed to it. The responsibility for contraception remained mainly with the man, however, with the condom (widely available since 1914) being the most commonly used method.

In 1961 the contraceptive pill was introduced in Britain and by 1964 half a million women were taking it. The pill gave women the choice of whether to become pregnant or not and brought a new found freedom into their lives. Within three years the Brook Centre in London was opening its doors to unmarried as well as married women, and in 1969 the Family Planning Act made such advice available to all women. This became free under the NHS in 1974.

SOURCE 17

The pill revolutionized contraception for women by giving them a totally reliable method ... which left them in control. Millions of women, both married and unmarried, enjoyed these benefits.

Historian, Sue Bruley, in Women in Britain since 1900

TASKS

1. Study Sources 15 and 16. Outline the main arguments used by campaigners for birth control advice in the 1920s and 1930s.

2. Discuss the opinion voiced by historian, Sue Bruley in Source 17. Could there be a counter-argument?

Reduction in the size of families

Due to improved advice on birth control, the introduction of the pill and changing attitudes among women regarding the importance of educational and employment opportunities, the size of families fell significantly during the twentieth century. The average family would have had 3.5 children in 1900; 2.3 children in the 1960s and 1.7 children in 1999. This pattern was interrupted only by the post Second World War 'baby boom' when young men returned home to their wives and wanted a 'normal' family life.

Abortion

Because of the lack of understanding and availability of reliable methods of birth control before the 1960s, there were many unwanted pregnancies among both unmarried and married women. In desperation many of these resorted to illegal means to get rid of their babies. Indeed, 20% of pregnancies in the 1920s ended in criminal abortions and in the 1930s they accounted for 35% of deaths among pregnant women in the Rhondda. Some of these abortions were self-induced by swallowing pills obtained through newspaper advertisements or through home operations with knitting needles or crochet hooks. Others were performed by illegal back-street abortionists, often with terrible consequences to the mothers' health.

The main campaigner for legal abortion on demand for all women was Stella Browne (1880-1955), who believed that the decision to terminate a pregnancy was a woman's right. Her slogan was 'Our bodies are our own'. The Abortion Law Reform Association was established in 1936 and two years later a prominent surgeon, Dr Aleck Bourne, was acquitted by the courts for performing an abortion on a 14 year old, whose life was in danger.

The momentum for change increased after the war and in 1967 the Abortion Act was passed. This allowed termination at up to 28 weeks, if two registered doctors agreed that the continuation of the pregnancy would damage the mental or physical health of the mother, or if there was a substantial risk of mental or physical handicap in the unborn child. The number of abortions rose rapidly in the 1970s, but the service provided by the NHS varied enormously from county to county in Wales, even in the 1980s. Some mothers had to pay for operations in private clinics.

SOURCE 18

Clwyd:	33%	Dyfed:	78%	Gwent:	54%
Gwynedd:	56%	Mid-Glamorgan:	56%	Powys:	55%
West Glamorgan:	94%	South Glamorgan:	36%		

Percentages of mothers receiving abortions on the NHS in the eight Welsh counties in 1982

This Act caused great controversy as church groups and many others believed that abortion kills unborn children. The debate continues today (the Act was amended to a termination at up to 24 weeks in 1990), and anti-abortionists such as the Pro-life Alliance continue to campaign vigorously against abortion.

A National Abortion Campaign protest in favour of abortion, 1979

Anti-abortion protestors marking the 40th anniversary of the 1967 Act

As far as I am concerned, men and women will never be equal until every child is a wanted child. I have yet to meet a woman who enjoyed an abortion. Abortion is the last resort.

Dot Clancy, Hackney, London, writing in the 1950s

TASKS

1. Using Source 18 consider the implications of these statistics for pregnant women in Wales in the 1980s.

2. Study Sources 19-21. Why do you think the issue of abortion has caused so much debate?

The issue of divorce

Until the 1960s divorce was a taboo subject in Wales and England. Divorced wives were particularly stigmatised because many believed they brought great shame upon themselves and their families. Before 1882 a married woman had to give up all rights to her own property and even to her own earnings and her husband could seek a divorce on grounds of adultery (being unfaithful) and keep full custody of the children. This changed gradually in the twentieth century when acts of parliament were passed to give wives also the right to divorce their husbands on grounds of adultery (1923), and on grounds of cruelty or desertion (1937), and when women were allowed to keep half the money saved from their housekeeping allowance (1964).

Yet even in the 1960s a woman could not take out a mortgage or buy items through **hire-purchase** without having a male guarantor (sponsor) to sign on her behalf.

In the meantime during the war years marriages had been disrupted, families divided and women had enjoyed some sense of independence while their husbands were away. As a result, the numbers of divorces in Wales and England rose dramatically from 8,000 in 1939 to 60,000 in 1947. In Wales, while there had been only 628 divorced women in 1931, by 1951 there were 4,935. In view of this the Marriage Law Reform Society was established in 1946.

In spite of opposition from the Roman Catholic Church and the Mothers' Union in the Church in Wales, who believed in the sanctity of marriage, the Divorce Reform Act was passed in 1969. A divorce could now be obtained if there had been an 'irretrievable breakdown' of marriage. Most importantly, it took away the stigma of blame from both parties. Leo Abse, MP for Pontypool, was instrumental in the passing of this reform.

SOURCE 22

By the mid-1960s – even though marriage itself remained popular – it was obvious that divorce was not going to go away.

There were too many suffering wives who, like my mother, were part of the first wave of women who thought: "This isn't what I want from a marriage and I'm not putting up with it."

When even the Church of England found fault in a law that forced couples into pointing the finger of blame at each other, it was clearly time for change.

The 1969 Divorce Reform Act has had as deep a social impact as any of the big liberal reform acts of the 1960s. Fault was removed from divorce and many people were able to get out of marriages that just were not working.

Kirsty Young, television presenter, in the BBC series
The British Family (January 2010)

SOURCE 23

" DON'T LEAVE ME, HELEN! CAN'T WE TALK ABOUT IT AFTER THE GOLF TOURNAMENT ? "

www.CartoonStock.com

SOURCE 24

Year	Number	Rate per 1000 marriages
1950	30,870	·
1960	23,868	·
1970	58,239	5.9
1980	148,301	12
1990	153,386	13
2000	141,135	12.7
2010	119,589	11.1

Divorce numbers and rates soared, peaking at 180,000 in 1993

Since 1970, therefore, the traditional nuclear family, with a husband and wife with dependent children has changed fundamentally. Marriage itself was officially at its lowest rate for over a hundred years in 2010 with only 20% of single adults choosing to get married. **Co-habitation** and re-marriage after divorcing have become much more common and acceptable.

TASK

Explain why there have been important changes in family patterns in recent times.

Single parenthood

The changing nature of marriage and society greatly increased the number of single parent households in Wales and England, either through death, divorce, separation or births outside marriage. In 1991, single parent families made up 13% of all the families in Wales; 93% of these were headed by single mothers. In 2006 nearly a quarter of the children in Wales and England lived with one parent only. Many of the single mothers found that combining parenthood and work was difficult and working part-time could mean the loss of vital benefit payments.

There has also been an increase in teenage pregnancies with the rate per 1000 in Wales in 1999 at 51, whilst the rate in England was 44. In more deprived areas the rate was even higher: at 65 per 1000 births in Rhondda Cynon Taf.

SOURCE 25

A study of five hundred south Wales schoolgirls in the late 1980s found that decisions about the future were constrained by an anticipation of becoming a mother, in a way that limited aspirations for education and training.

Sociologist Teresa Rees describing the limited horizons of many south Wales schoolgirls, in her article 'Women in Post-War Wales'

SOURCE 26

increasing numbers of young women in Wales appear to be opting for the role of unmarried mother ... Lone motherhood at least offers the prospect of housing, adult status and a minimal income (Rees and Winckler, 1986; Windsor, 1984). It is however an adult status in a domestic capacity and an income still derived through dependence, albeit on the state rather than on a partner.

Rees, T. and Winckler, V. (1986) 'Last Hired, First Fired?', *Planet: The Welsh Internationalist*, 57, pp. 38-41
Windsor, P. (1984) *Out of Sight: A Study of Young Women's Lives on a Swansea Estate*, Swansea: Youth Enterprise

Historian Victoria Winckler in her article 'Women and Work in Contemporary Wales', 1987

Thus many single female parent families have exchanged dependency upon husbands and male bread-winners with dependency upon the state. Although there is now a National Council for One Parent Families, it is largely the extended network of other women in the family who provide the necessary supporting systems to help such single parent mothers.

TASKS

1. Study Sources 25 and 26. Suggest why the number of single-parent families has risen in Wales and England since the Second World War.

2. What challenges do single parents face?

This section provides guidance on how to answer question 1(c) from units 1 and 2. It is a source analysis and evaluation question and can relate to a visual or written source. It is worth 5 marks.

Question 1(c) – analysis and evaluation of a source and the recall of own knowledge

How far does Source A support the view that the lives of women were improved by the introduction of family allowance in 1946?

[5 marks]

SOURCE A

Almost all thought of them [Family Allowances] as an effort to boost the birthrate, rather than as an amelioration [improvemen] of hardship for the more prolific. They were taken as an inducement, a bribe, a payment – and a very inadequate one: 'the wife said *she* wasn't going to have a baby for five bob a week'. 'I'd like to see *them* keep a baby on five shillings'.

From E. Slater and M. Woodside, Patterns of Marriage, *(1951)*

Tips on how to answer

● If it is a visual source you should aim to **pick out relevant details** from what you can see in the illustration and, equally importantly, from the caption that supports the source. It is useful to scribble notes around the source.

● If it is a written source you should **underline or highlight** the key points.

● In your answer you should use these details, explaining them **in your own words** and linking them directly to the question.

● You should bring in **your own knowledge** of this topic to expand upon these points and to provide additional material that is not provided in the source.

● To obtain maximum marks you must remember to give a **reasoned judgement** that addresses the question. E.g.: 'This source does/does not support the view that ... because ...'

Candidate response

The source disagrees with the view that the introduction of family allowances improved the lives of women. The Source shows the attitude of working class women who saw family allowances as a very unsatisfactory payment. Five shillings would in no way help working class women to bring up a child. They would be out of pocket overall. The Source is from an official study and only shows the attitude of working class women. What it doesn't show is how other groups of richer women might have felt about family allowances. The source therefore does not support the view that family allowance improved the lives of women.

The candidate discusses the content of the source with an attempt at a reasoned judgement on the set question. The candidate has made some speculative observations using the attribution of the source. However, the candidate has not expanded on the content of the source by providing key details and background knowledge. On balance this response is level 2 work and worthy of 3 marks.

Now you have a go

How far does Source B support the view that the lives of women were improved by the introduction of the National Health Service?

[5 marks]

SOURCE B

A photograph of a medical clinic for expectant mothers and toddlers in Caernarfon, 1951

HOW HAVE CHANGES IN HOME AND FAMILY LIFE IN RECENT TIMES AFFECTED WOMEN IN WALES AND ENGLAND?

Introduction

SOURCE 1

A cartoon by Viv Quillin (1946-)

TASKS

1. What does this cartoon tell us about improvements in housing in the post-war period?

2. What does it tell us about women's work in the home in the same period?

IMPROVEMENTS IN HOUSING

After the Second World War (1939-45), there was a serious shortage of houses in Britain. 200,000 houses had been destroyed by bombs and millions had been partially damaged. In 1946, 40,000 families lived in temporary camps built originally, as in the village of Llan-non in Ceredigion, to house prisoners of war. There were also still many slum areas in Britain. Even in 1956, 55,000 houses in Liverpool were listed as unfit for people to live in. This situation affected women in particular because they still spent far more of their time in the home than men. After the upheaval of the war years, women were encouraged to return to unpaid work in the home and to resume their places as wives and mothers. Only a quarter of Welsh women, for example, were engaged in paid work in 1951. In this period too, marriages soared, but married couples had to share rooms or apartments with other couples or with relatives. Others had to squat in empty buildings until housing became available.

SOURCE 2

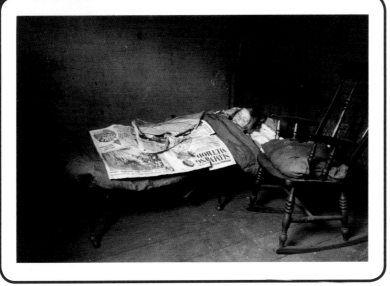

A child sleeping in a Liverpool slum in 1956

TASK

What does Source 2 suggest about living conditions in the slum areas in the 1950s?

The Beveridge Report of 1942 (see pp. 15-16) had identified 'Squalor' (filth because of poverty), as one of the 'Five Evil Giants' that had to be conquered in the post-war era. Several different solutions were attempted during the next decades.

One immediate answer the government introduced in 1946 was the 'Temporary Housing Programme' – a programme to construct houses produced in packs in factories. These houses were called **pre-fabs**, and they arrived on the back of a lorry, ready to be assembled. Four types of materials were used: steel, asbestos, wood and aluminium, but aluminium proved the most popular. By 1949, when the programme came to an end, 156,000 pre-fabs had been built in Britain, 7,000 of them in Wales. They were detached and surrounded by their own strip of garden. These houses, with their built-in cupboards and stainless steel kitchen units, were well equipped with electricity, running hot and cold water and even central heating. Although built as an emergency measure to last ten years, some people still lived in pre-fabs fifty years later.

SOURCE 3

Pre-fab houses in Neath c. 1950

Mrs Kitty Williams of Cardigan was delighted when she moved to a pre-fab after the war. She had spent a miserable year in 'rooms', sharing a kitchen and bathroom with another family. The pre-fab was 'lovely' and the rent was only £1 a week. 'You'd say from seeing it from the outside ... "Oh dear, what an old shed", but if you went in ... "Oh!"'

Mrs Kitty Williams, Cardigan, recorded in 2001 for the oral history project 'Hanes Merched Cymru (The History of Women in Wales), 1920-60'

Study Sources 3 and 4 and the information provided. What were the advantages and disadvantages of pre-fab homes?

Larger post-war housing

The main solution proposed by the post-war Labour government was the building of council houses. Aneurin Bevan (see p. 15) was appointed the Minister for Health and Housing and his aim was to get the county councils to build high-quality houses to rent out to working class tenants. Three million new council houses were built in Britain in the 1950s. In Wales between 1945 and 1951 an average of 8,250 houses were built ever year – 87% of these were council houses; whilst between 1951 and 1964 the average was 13,500 a year, with 63% of them council houses. Bevan raised the minimum size for a council house from 70 square metres to 93 square metres, so that they were spacious. They also had their own big gardens, three bedrooms, a bathroom and a kitchen, with hot water on tap. Coal-fires still provided the heating.

For Mareth Lewis of Llanelli, who had suffered a breakdown after getting married in 1949, because of the discomfort of living in shared rooms, moving to a council house was like moving to Buckingham Palace! (She was recorded in 2001 for the oral history project *Hanes Merched Cymru 1920-60 [The History of Women in Wales]*). Because of the demand, there were long waiting lists for these houses and a great deal of anger when some people managed to jump the queue, because they were related to a local councillor. Council house building continued for over twenty years. Queen's Park estate (now called Caia Park) in Wrexham was laid out in the early 1950s to plans by the influential town planner and architect Gordon Stephenson and the Gurnos estate in Merthyr Tydfil was the largest in Europe, when it was built in the 1960s. However, there was a tendency to build the larger council estates on the outskirts of towns and, because of a lack of local amenities, many problems occurred. The huge Penrhys council estate, built between 1966-8, on the mountain-top between the valleys of the Rhondda Fawr and the Rhondda Fach, was regarded initially as a desirable place to live. Indeed, the houses were among the first in the Valleys to have central heating. Very soon, however, the reality of living 1000 feet above sea level and the incessant rain changed the inhabitants' attitudes. The fabric of the houses began to deteriorate and serious social problems developed. Such conditions and difficulties would have had a very negative effect on the women, and especially the young mothers, abandoned on such estates day after day.

In the 1980s council house building almost came to an end and the occupiers were encouraged to buy their properties.

People today do not realize the sheer joy it was for a family in the post-war years to move into a council house with all its 'mod cons'. ... The house was semi-detached with three bedrooms, two good-sized downstairs rooms, a well designed modern kitchen complete with gas cooker, a gas boiler for washing clothes and a pantry ... We had an upstairs bathroom and toilet.

Hilda Price, born in 1920 in Cadoxton, Barry

[It was] found that a move away from cramped accommodation to a council estate, although welcomed, could mean renewed and greater anxieties, and caused considerable strain ... where the higher rent could only be paid by skimping on food and other necessities.

Conclusions of a small survey of 59 mothers by the Christian Economic and Social Research Foundation, 1957

TASK

Would you agree that Sources 5 and 6 contradict each other? Could they both be accurate? Explain your answer.

Another aspect of the post-war building programme was the designation and creation of new towns, with their car-orientated layout and shopping centres. Among those built in England were Stevenage, Basildon and Milton Keynes and in Wales, Cwmbrân, in the southeast and Newtown in Powys were identified as new towns. Today Cwmbrân is the sixth largest urban area in Wales with a population of around 50,000.

When building land was scarce, another solution had to be found for the housing problem. During the 1950s and 60s in particular, councils decided to demolish what were considered to be slum areas and build high-rise flats in their place. These flats were quite luxurious, but once again social problems developed when lifts broke down and people began to feel isolated and removed from their old communities. One of the most famous tower block developments was the Parkhill Flats development in Sheffield, built in 1960. These 'streets in the sky' were built to replace the grim terraces bulldozed after the war and to give families indoor toilets, central heating and airy balconies. At first, the families couldn't believe their luck – they loved their modern new homes. But as the buildings began to show cracks, it wasn't long before residents started to throw their rubbish over the balconies, and Parkhill Flats became new slums. Although building upwards was the new, progressive future, and although most people wanted modern conveniences, they actually wanted them in nice little houses with nice little gardens. Likewise in Wales the new high-rise flats built in Dyfatti (Swansea), Newport, Cwmbrân and Butetown (Cardiff) were controversial too.

SOURCE 7

Houses being demolished in Butetown, Cardiff, while the new tower blocks of Loudon House and Nelson House rise up behind them; 1969

(i) I lived in Loudoun Square [Butetown] which had about 62 houses and about 42 nations (from 42 different countries) in them. We all got along with each other very well ... When they tore down the houses and ripped up the Square, they upset a community of lovely people.

(ii) The house is just falling down ... I often have to wear a coat and hat when I am working here (in the kitchen) ... giant rats run about the house taking the very food from the kitchen table

(iii) It's beautiful ... I love these flats. The only thing, it's like a gaol [prison], everyone locks their doors.

The oral testimonies of (i) Nora Glasgow, (ii) Mrs Crother (46 year old mother of 4), and (iii) Mrs Lilly Casser, all residents of Butetown, Cardiff in the 1960s

TASK

Write a short newspaper article about the change to living in high-rise flats and its impact upon women. Use the oral testimonies in Source 8 as quotations and the other information to help you.

During this period too, private builders were building houses in the suburbs of towns and cities. In Swansea the large new estates in Killay and Dunvant were built at this time, as were the sprawling estates in Waunfawr, Aberystwyth. Thus, private home ownership increased significantly in the United Kingdom, from 29% of all houses in 1950 to 51% in 1972.

Amenities and further improvements

By the 1950s and 60s every housewife wanted all the modern conveniences, or 'mod cons', available. These included electricity and electrical appliances, indoor bathrooms and toilets and central heating. But there was still a great way to go. By and large, electricity did not reach the farmhouses and cottages of rural Wales until the early 1950s, and even when it did, many families could not afford to buy electrical appliances. Certainly the coming of electricity to a village was an exciting and memorable event.

(i) Wiring the house cost us £150 – a fortune in those days. But what luxury!

(ii) I remember it was in 1957. ... I remember very well the thrill of feeling that our village was 'modern' at last.

(iii) Our council house was the lap of luxury after the cramped cottage. There were lights in every room, even in the toilet. Power points too ... but as yet, we were slow to use them.

The oral testimonies of (i) Mrs Glenys Roberts, Mold; (ii) Carys Briddon, Tre'r-Ddôl; and (iii) Joyce Roberts, Wrexham.

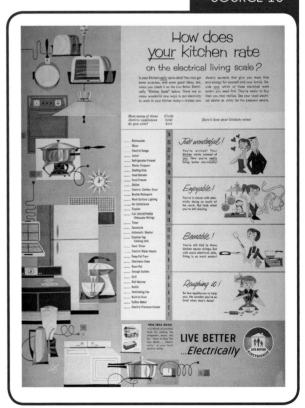

An important report called *Homes for Today and Tomorrow* by the Parker-Morris Committee in 1961 set high standards for housing and identified elements such as more electrical sockets, continuous work surfaces in kitchens and central heating, which would make homes more comfortable and efficient. Although some of the new houses built in the post-war period did have central heating, it was not a common feature of homes until the late 1970s. Even in 1986 50% of homes in Wales and England still did not have full central heating. Oil, gas and solid fuel were used to fuel these central heating systems. The use of gas for heating and cooking had increased greatly since the 1950s.

SOURCE 11

(i) Everybody did everything in the room where the fire was, in the winter. ... Going to the toilet was agony, it meant going out into the rest of the house, where it was always freezing.

(ii) Every room in our house was so cold. The kitchen with the range was the only really warm room; everywhere else had lino-covered floors ... It was like living in the Arctic Circle.

The oral testimonies of two interviewees in The Best of Times: Growing Up in Britain in the 1950s

Another major improvement was the installation of a hot water system and an indoor toilet and bathroom. Grants were distributed to 200,000 houses in Wales for such improvements.

SOURCE 12

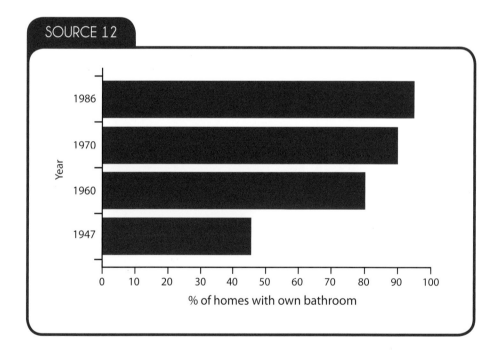

% of homes with own bathroom

TASKS

1. How useful are the oral testimonies quoted in Sources 9 and 11 to the historian studying housing in post-war Wales and England?

2. Why does the advertisement in Source 10 target female consumers in particular?

3. Explain the graph in Source 12 in your own words.

Labour-saving devices

Although most of the labour-saving devices had been invented before the war, it wasn't until there was a general supply of gas and electricity and electrical sockets that they became common fixtures in post-war homes. The order in which housewives secured the new electrical appliances, as they came to afford them, is interesting:

1. iron,
2. kettle,
3. fire,
4. vacuum cleaner,
5. cooker,
6. washing machine,
7. fridge.

Later, in the 1970s and 80s, food processors, microwave ovens, dishwashers and freezers became indicators of a modern home. Almost all the promotional material and advertisements developed to sell these appliances was aimed at women. Women became identified with the new domestic technology and were often pictured as eager consumers, determined to 'keep up with the Joneses'. Indeed some wives were proud to receive a food processor or a dishwasher as a Christmas present from their grateful husbands and families, although the appliance might be as relevant to the comfort of their lives as it was to hers!

A 1950s style single tub washing machine

A cartoon by Leslie Illingworth showing women with their hands full of consumer goods in 1954

The new domestic technology certainly speeded up housework, but many women today question whether it did, in fact, lessen the burden of housework. In some cases it could be argued that it added to that burden. Also, because women seemed to be less 'tied to the kitchen sink', they could be expected to be more than 'ordinary housewives'. With the introduction of more labour-saving devices in the home, there was an expectation that more married wives and mothers would go out to work. This, in turn, would enable them to buy further labour-saving devices.

Helped by the new gadgetry, economic security and benefiting from higher standards of housing, the 1950s housewife had been released from some of the worst drudgery of the past.

Historian Sue Bruley in Women in Britain since 1900 *(1999)*

Once you have carpets on the floor, you have to keep vacuuming them. Once you have acquired a twin tub washing machine ... the sheets and everything else get changed much more often and that makes more ironing.

Author Elaine Morgan (born in Pontypridd, in 1920), describes the new cares of the 1970s housewife

we should not exaggerate the impact of the electric appliances. ... Housework expands to fill the time available. But whichever way we view the issue, owning a vacuum cleaner certainly did not give women 'equality'.

Historian Deirdre Beddoe's comments on the impact of new technology (2000)

TASKS

1. What were the main advances in domestic technology in the post-war period? What does the cartoon in Source 14 suggest about them?

2. Study Sources 15-17. Compare and contrast the comments regarding the impact of the new appliances upon women as home-makers.

One aspect that has been very slow to change, in spite of the fact that men are usually portrayed as being good with gadgets and technology, is their attitudes towards sharing the burden and responsibilities of doing the housework. In 1977, husbands did less than half the housework done by their wives and in a survey by the United Kingdom government in 1986, most married people believed that women should do most of the washing, ironing, cooking and cleaning. Some women began a 'Wages for Housework Campaign' in 1972, arguing that women's unwaged work in the home was worth millions of pounds to the economy every year and that they should be financially compensated for it. Others felt that the only solution was to get men to accept their responsibilities fully.

No mass campaign, or local authority provision, or legal reform, can make individual men behave fairly at home if they don't want to and if individual *women* won't, can't or daren't insist.

... Sex equality in the home will not on its own solve the housework problem. But there can be no solution without it.

Author Zoë Fairbairns in 1988

TASK

What were the main arguments of the 'Wages for Housework Campaign' and the response of the author of Source 18?

Energy-efficient modern homes

In the early twenty-first century a great deal of emphasis has been placed upon making homes as **energy-efficient** as possible, in order to be more environmentally friendly and to reduce carbon emissions. But as early as 1973, in Wales, the Centre for Alternative Technology (CAT) had been opened in a disused slate quarry near Machynlleth in Powys.

This eco-centre provided information on all aspects of sustainable living, including solar, wind and hydropower; how to build low-energy houses and the construction of straw bale and rammed earth buildings. Many of their innovative ideas have become accepted as good practice in this century.

Grants have been made available for installing solar panels to produce electricity from natural sunlight, and for cavity wall and loft insulation. Double-glazed windows and doors have become almost the norm and energy-efficient light bulbs also contribute to reducing the 'carbon footprint'. All electrical appliances are expected to be more energy-efficient and they are rated accordingly. For example, the most energy-efficient washing machine would be AA rated – A for spin efficiency and A for wash performance. Rather than use a tumble dryer, which uses a great deal of electricity, families are encouraged to dry their washing outdoors in the traditional way on old-fashioned clothes lines.

In 2011 Wrexham Borough Council announced a £60 million project to fit 3,000 council houses with solar panels. The county's carbon footprint would be reduced by c. 3,000 tonnes of CO_2 every year.

Solar panels on the roof of a modern home

In 2010 the government stated that the Code for Sustainable Homes, calling for newly built homes to reach Level 3 (out of 6) on carbon emissions, should be applied. By 2050 the target is for all households in Britain to be at Level 6, with zero emissions.

INCREASED FREE TIME

With the various improvements in the home and in health and family life in the second half of the twentieth century, women had more time and money to spend on leisure activities. Yet, it would be incorrect to picture life before the Second World War as lacking in any free time and entertainment. Chapels and churches with their sisterhoods, Mothers' Unions, prayer meetings and social activities were central to many women's lives and have remained so into the twenty-first century. The majority of regular cinema and theatre-goers were, and are, women. The cinema's ability to transport the viewer into another world, often one of romance far removed from the harsh realities of daily life, had a special appeal to women in particular. On the hearth, knitting and sewing were not only necessary skills to clothe the family, but also a source of pride and enjoyment. The Women's Institute, founded in Llanfair Pwllgwyngyll, Anglesey, in 1915, originally to revitalise rural communities, has organized regular meetings throughout Wales and England to discuss all kinds of issues of interest to women during the twentieth century.

SOURCE 20

(i) It was a small chapel, one floor, but – it was everything to us. ... We spent all our time there. Going there was like going home.

(ii) You had to go to chapel, didn't you? ... At that time everybody went there, and if you didn't go, you were left out.

The oral testimonies of (i) Valerie James, Brynaman and (ii) Ellen Vaughan Ellis, Fourcrosses, Pwllheli, speaking about the 1940s and 50s. (recorded for the Hanes Merched Cymru [Welsh Women's History] 1920-60 oral history project)

SOURCE 21

The Women's Institute's support for the Keep Britain Tidy campaign in 1955

TASK

Through oral history do your own research into women's formal and informal leisure activities in the twentieth century.

The impact of women's magazines

Before the Second World War there were over 50 magazines aimed specifically at women. They were immensely popular, selling millions of copies throughout Wales and England every week or month. The titles and the covers of these magazines often emphasised the doctrine of domestic ideology, depicting women in what was seen as their primary role in society, working in the home; e.g. *Woman and Home, Homes and Gardens, My Home* and *Good Housekeeping*, aimed at the middle class; while *Woman's Weekly*'s mission was to celebrate the home and family life. *Woman's Own* (1932) and *Woman* (1937) targeted working class women.

These magazines remained immensely popular in post-war Wales and England and many are still among the high sellers in the twenty-first century. Since the 1970s, however, they have moved away from articles based purely on domestic life. Although they still feature recipes, fashion and modern homes, they also discuss difficult health issues, careers and real life-stories. They have responded to the demand for features on harder topics, such as divorce, abortion and domestic violence and can be said to have helped educate a mass audience of women about these important issues. The over-riding change, however, has been the increase in magazines that celebrate celebrity culture and what is perceived to be the insatiable desire of women to read about such celebrities. The list of best-selling magazines in Wales and England illustrates the variety of magazines available to women in 2011 and their popularity:

Two pre-war women's magazine covers showing women as housewives

Name	Circulation per week / month in 2011	Brief description
OK!	473,167	Established 1993; celebrity news, fashion and entertainment …
Good Housekeeping	430,878	Est. 1922 in Britain; product testing, diet, recipes and health …
Hello	413,311	Est. 1988, celebrity life-style, royalty and entertainment …
Cosmopolitan (Cosmo)	386,852	A product of the 1960s – hard-hitting feminist in outlook; relationships, self-improvement, careers, fashion …
Woman and Home	370,284	Diet and well-being, fashion, for 35+ women
Slimming World	349,566	Associated with the organisation of the same name – diet and health
Woman's Weekly	339,993	Knitting patterns, recipes, crafts, well-being
Heat	326,677	Est. 1999, gossip-orientated, celebrity stories, beauty advice …
Woman	286,890	Est. 1934 for 30-40 year old women; body-confident fashion
Prima	280,207	Crafts, holidays, cooking, 'Sew a union jack cushion'

As shown in Source 23, the magazine *Cosmopolitan* (*Cosmo*) took a more feminist approach to women's lives. But the really hard-hitting magazines, which were associated with the Women's Liberation Movement, were *Spare Rib* and the radical feminist American *Ms*, launched in 1971. These dealt with such topics as sex trafficking, the wage gap, the glass ceiling and domestic violence. The magazine *Rhiannon*, which appeared first in 1977, was a Welsh feminist publication containing both Welsh and English language articles.

Two issues of the bilingual feminist magazine Rhiannon, *1979*

Several Welsh language women's magazines were published during the twentieth century too. *Y Gymraes* (the Welshwoman), edited by Alice Gray Jones, or 'Ceridwen Peris', was religious in tone, but it did encourage women to take an active part in public life. Two other magazines appeared in the 1960s and 70s: *Hon* (This One) (1963-), a sophisticated magazine mainly for middle class and professional women, and *Pais*, (Petticoat) (1978-91), primarily intended for young women and mothers. Both were well received but were not able to sustain sales for a long period. *Y Wawr* (The Dawn), the magazine of the Welsh language women's movement *Merched y Wawr* (*Daughters of the Dawn*), launched in 1968, on the other hand, through its careful mix of articles about travel, influential Welsh women, health issues, and current Welsh language matters, tries to fulfil the demand for a Welsh language magazine for all Welsh-speaking women in Wales.

Hon, *Welsh-language women's magazine, Autumn 1963 showing its elegant modern design*

Y Wawr, *Welsh-language magazine for women, Spring 2011*

TASK

Research 2 different current women's magazines. Make a list of their contents. How would you describe them? (e.g. traditional, feminist, outward looking, controversial)

Radio and television programmes

Between 1923 and 1939, the number of radio sets in Britain rose from 200,000 to nine million. Television, on the other hand did not really take off until after the Second World War and even in 1951 only 9% of British homes owned a television set. Colour television was introduced in 1969 and by 2001 97.5% of households had at least one television in the home.

Radio and television have been important media for women during the twentieth century. Often they have reinforced the notion that women's lives are centred on the home. Yet, there have been relatively few programmes explicitly targeting women listeners or viewers. The long running radio programme, *Women's Hour*, first broadcast in 1946 on BBC Radio Light Programme and transferred to Radio 4 in 1973, has enjoyed considerable success and has succeeded in adjusting its content and style to match the changing times. In the beginning, with a male producer and presenter, housewives were bombarded with household hints and recipes, but today it tackles all kinds of controversial issues and other less contentious stories that are of interest to women. On television, ITV's *Loose Women* is a recent attempt at capturing the female audience, which is at home during the day, but its presenters have been branded by feminists as 'magazine reading, cupcake making, accessory-buying fluff'.

In mainstream programmes, although women have made their mark as newsreaders in the newsrooms, men still dominate the heavyweight news programmes. In 2010 84% of the reporters and guests on *Today* (Radio 4's morning news programme) and 72% of contributors to *Question Time* (BBC1/BBC2), for example, were men.

In the Welsh language media there have been programmes such as *Merched yn Bennaf* (Mostly for Women, in the 1980s) on the radio and *Hamdden* (Leisure, 1970s) and *Hon* (This One, 2000s) on television, which have been aimed primarily at the female market. They have tried to represent a whole range of issues that are of particular concern to women.

Moira Stuart was the first African-Caribbean female national television newsreader in 1981

> **TASK**
>
> Listen to or watch a news programme of your choice on radio or television. Count the number of male / female presenters and contributors. Work out the percentages and compare them with the figures given above.

Fitness and leisure advice

In the early twentieth century only middle and upper class women would have had the time and energy to participate in organized physical activities. Schools and colleges did run hockey, netball and other team sports, but only the exceptionally talented continued to play in leagues and tournaments into adulthood. During the 1930s, however, there was a great deal of interest in physical exercise for both men and women. In 1930 Mary Bagot-Stack founded the 'Women's League of Health and Beauty', based upon the motto 'movement for life'. Fitness was seen not as an end in itself, but as a means of enhancing both physical and mental wellbeing. It aimed at appealing to a wide spectrum of women and classes were held in village halls, shops and factories. By 1939 it had over 170,000 members and it was a worldwide organization. Prunella Stack carried on the work after her mother's death in 1935. The Fitness League is still an active movement today.

TASK

Search for <u>British League of Health and Beauty</u> on the Internet and watch Video 1 by British Pathé.

During and immediately after the Second World War, organized physical exercises for women were not prioritised. Indeed, due to modern technology, many women were leading much more inactive lifestyles both in work and in the home. Then, in the late 1960s and 70s specialist Sports Centres were built, where women could join aerobic, yoga and keep fit classes and take advantage of the swimming pools and spa facilities.

A decade later pioneers such as Rosemary Conley and Jane Fonda introduced these exercises into the home environment by producing fitness videos, and morning television programmes showing exercises with 'The Green Goddess', for example, became very popular.

SOURCE 27

Rosemary Conley's Inch Loss Plan

SOURCE 28

A fitness session in a women-only gym, 2010

In recent years there has been a demand for 'women only' gyms, especially from women who want to exercise but whose religion does not allow them to do so in the presence of men. Women now participate in activities such as circuit training sessions, boot camps, kickboxing, zumba dancing and buggyfit classes for new mothers.

There is a vast range of fitness, health and well-being advice available in bookshops, on DVDs and websites today, including advice for pregnant mothers, women over 40 and those suffering from osteoporosis. In spite of all this advice, it was recorded in 2008-09 that nearly a quarter of UK women – 23.9% – were obese, while one in every hundred women between 15 and 30 suffered from the eating disorder, anorexia nervosa.

All this evidence demonstrates that during the twentieth century, there has been a very significant change in the balance between housework, paid work and leisure time in women's lives and in the very nature of those activities in Wales and England.

TASK

From the information provided in this section, write a few lines to compare and contrast the kind of fitness exercises popular before the Second World War and afterwards.

Examination practice

This section provides guidance on how to answer question 1(e) from Units 1 and 2. The question deals with historical interpretation through analysis, evaluation and cross referencing of two sources.

Question 1(e) – explain differences in historical interpretation

Why do Sources A and B have different views about women at home?

[8 marks]

These two sources say different things about women at home by the end of the twentieth century.

SOURCE A

British males have gone from "Mad Men" to "Yes Men" in the last few decades when it comes to doing [household] chores, a new survey claims. ...

The average man of the house has increased the amount of time he spends on domestic duties by more than 60 per cent over the past 30 years, according to research. ...

For women, this is easing the burden of cooking, cleaning and getting the children to bed.

From an article in The Daily Telegraph, *a British newspaper, July 31st 2011*

SOURCE B

Within the home ... there has been no fundamental redistribution of domestic tasks between men and women. A tiny minority of men have opted to be house-husbands ... More generally ... everyday household tasks – cooking, cleaning, washing and ironing and child-care – remain women's responsibility.

Deirdre Beddoe in Out of the Shadows *2000 p. 178*

Tips on how to answer:

You need to refer to the **content of both** sources, relate this to your **own knowledge** of this period and consider the attributions. This will require you to perform a thorough evaluation of both sources.

- You need to read through both sources with care, **underlining** or **highlighting** the important details. You can also scribble some **notes in the margin** around the source about how it fits into your knowledge of the period.

- Does it confirm what you know?

- Does it only refer to part of the answer and are some important points missing?

- Does it agree or disagree with what is said in the other source?

- This will enable you to **compare and contrast** the two sources in terms of their content value.

- You now need to consider the **origin** of each source, saying who the authors are and when they made their observations. E.g. Are they primary or secondary?

- You should then consider the **purpose** of each source, noting the **circumstances** under which they were written. E.g. Is the source written by a modern historian or a contemporary? Does the author display a biased point of view and if so why?

- To obtain maximum marks you need to produce a **balanced** answer with **good support** from both sources and your own knowledge, together with a **detailed consideration of the attributions** of each source.

Response by candidate one

Source A is from a British newspaper. It says that men have increased the amount of time that they spend on household tasks. In the last 30 years they have increased the time they spend on domestic duties by 60%. Source B is written by Deidre Beddoe, who is an historian who is writing about the role of women. She says that little has changed for women in the home. Although a few men have become house husbands.

Examiner's comment

This is a weak answer that simply paraphrases the content of the sources. This is a generalised answer that makes no clear attempt to address the set question about why there are differences between the two views shown about women in the home. This answer would be at level 1 and only be credited with 2 marks.

Response by candidate two

The sources give very different views of women in the home. Source A is a newspaper report which was published in 2011. It suggests that men have changed their attitude to household tasks and have become 'Yes men'. This has meant that the burden upon women has been lifted and that there is greater equality in the home as a result. I would expect a newspaper like 'The Telegraph' to be accurate because it is not a tabloid newspaper but a more respected broadsheet. However, newspapers sometimes exaggerate storylines in order to attract readers and make more money. The references to: 'Mad Men to Yes Men' is typical of such journalism. Source B has a different viewpoint from Source A. It comes from a book about the role of women. Source B says that there is no significant improvement in the lives of women in the home. The burden of house work still falls upon women. The author is a historian who would have researched the topic well and the information is likely to be balanced and informed.

Considers the content and standpoint expressed in Source A

Considers the content and standpoint expressed in Source B

Published in 2000, Beddoe would have had time to consult a range of evidence to produce a balanced account. However, she has collected evidence that largely overlooks any improvements, such as labour saving devices, better housing and improved services, which women have seen in their domestic life. This may be because she may well be writing from the angle of a feminist, and so this may be a distorted view of women in the home. Source B tells a very different story to that provided in Source A. The two sources say opposite things about women in the home and this is due to the circumstances under which they were produced. Source A is produced to create an effect on the readers, building up a story to make it appear more important than it actually was. Source B was written by a person who is obviously supporting the feminist position on women in the home. Both sources take an almost extreme position on the issue of women in the home, and I have doubts about their reliability.

> Compares the two sources and tries to explain the differences

Examiner's response

This is a developed answer. There are clear references to content and the circumstances under which each was produced. The content has been explained and put into context. There is good consideration of both attributions. The concluding paragraph compares and contrasts both sources and does offer a judgement, which although unnecessary is welcomed.

The answer reaches the highest level and scores 8 marks.

Now you have a go

Why do Sources C and D have different views about women at home?

[8 marks]

SOURCE C

Caroline Spelman (Member of Parliament for Meriden and Secretary of State for the Department of Environment, Food and Rural Affairs. 2012)

Women have drawn the short straw: we have increasing equality at work but little progress on equal load-bearing at home. Just ask who matches the socks, folds the washing, stocks the fridge, and does the mending and all in her spare time!

From Banishing the Myths: Fawcett Society Annual Report 2000-2001, *p.10*

SOURCE D

[From the 1960s onwards] housework became easier and quicker. Housewives were liberated from the time-consuming, repetitive, labour intensive work involved in the home, particularly cooking, laundry work and house cleaning.

W.Gareth Evans, an historian writing in a GCSE history text book, The Changing Role and Status of Women in the Twentieth Century, *(2000), p.81*

CHAPTER 4

HOW WERE WOMEN EMPLOYED IN THE EARLY TWENTIETH CENTURY IN WALES AND ENGLAND

Introduction

SOURCE 1

Grouped Occupations	Males	Females
Mines, quarries, brick-making	1471	–
Food and drink (making and selling)	2532	1739
Iron, steel and tinplate	5573	472
Engineering and vehicles	3585	33
Clothes (Making and selling)	1447	2523
Building and construction	3293	–
Transport (+ railways and docks)	8521	–
Professional	1196	931
Domestic service	328	3897

Extract from the 1911 Census showing the occupations of workers aged 10 or over in Swansea Borough Council

TASKS

1. What does Source 1 tell us about how men and women were employed at the beginning of the twentieth century?

2. What other information would be useful before you could use this confidently as a historical source?

TRADITIONAL EMPLOYMENT

It is very difficult to know how many women were in paid work and exactly what work they did at the beginning of the twentieth century. The main sources historians use are the census returns every ten years. However, women often worked part-time, or did casual or **seasonal work** and did not regard this work as important enough to be declared at all. Also many women worked in their family businesses – in shops or on farms and once again these are not counted in the census figures. Married women might take in lodgers or washing, but the data does not mention these aspects either.

Taking these problems into consideration, the census figures for Wales do suggest that only 23.6% of women were in paid work in 1911, while in England the percentage was 32.8%. This reflects the fact that in Wales, heavy industry (coal, iron and steel) destroyed women's jobs. The percentage participation rate for the Rhondda, for example, was only 14.4%; while in Ceredigion it was 30%.

Domestic service

The traditional occupation of single women at this time was in **domestic service**. According to the 1901 census, 50.7% of the women who did paid work in Wales were in domestic service, compared with 40.3% in England. Domestic service was regarded as the most suitable job for young women and an ideal training for future working class wives. These maidservants could be in service in large mansions as part of the 'downstairs' team (see Chapter 1), in middle and working class households and on farms. In middle class households one or two maids-of-all-work would be hired – they were the lowest on the social scale and the experience was often one of drudgery and loneliness. Many working class girls emigrated from Wales to Liverpool and London to seek work in their fellow-Welshmen's middle class homes.

On large farms there would be a hierarchy of maidservants, for example: the senior maid, the kitchen maid, who milked and churned and fed the calves, and the junior maid, at everyone's beck and call. They would all be under the constant supervision of the farm mistress. They lived in the farmhouse itself and could be called upon to work at any time. These maids would be hired by the year and since they received their food and lodging, their pay was little more than pocket money.

Farm work could be rough and unpleasant and maidservants would be expected to help outdoors with the harvest, during shearing and with muck-spreading and clearing stones according to the season. In most cases these maids left their employment when they got married.

The textile trades

In England, the textile industry – in the cotton and woollen mills of Lancashire and Yorkshire in particular – employed many thousands of married and unmarried women. In this period the school leaving age was 12 and young girls were prized in the mills for their nimble fingers. The working conditions were very unhealthy. The cotton mills were hot and humid and the workers suffered from lung diseases and TB due to the cotton dust and eye and skin infections. Because of the noise levels from over 500 looms in the weaving shops, the women had to learn to lip read and deafness was common.

Women weavers at the Cockhedge Cotton Works, Warrington, Lancashire, with the male bosses on the side, looking on. In this mill the women worked from 6.00 a.m. until 5.30 p.m. Monday to Friday and Saturday until 12 noon. If they were caught talking they would be sent home and their pay would be docked

In Wales too there were 7,358 woollen and hosiery workers in 1911, a high percentage of whom were women. The Teifi valley factories at Drefach Felindre and those in the Newtown area of mid-Wales were particularly important. Wages were usually between nine shillings (45p) and fifteen shillings (75p) a week. In the large Pryce Jones Mills in Newtown, Powys, which had a large mail-order business, a programme of lectures, concerts and dances was organized for the employees.

Tinplate workers in Swansea in the 1900s

Other occupations

The metal industries, which included the flourishing tinplate works in Morriston, Gorseinon and Llanelli in south Wales, employed about 3,525 women, mostly in the least skilled and worst paid jobs. They worked as separators, separating plates of tin, which were stuck together after the rolling process, with a machete-like tool called a hanger. This was dangerous work and workers had to bandage their hands to protect them.

my mother was working for a week ... for six shillings [30p] ... and handling weight, and the heat of the tinworks ... working like men. Coming home – you could see them taking their shirts and dress off, and squeezing the perspiration out of them.

The oral testimony of Cecil Lewis, born in Morriston in 1913, recalling his mother, who worked in the tinplate works

Some women were employed in heavy labour on the surface in coalmines, in brickworks and in the docks of Cardiff during this period too.

Dressmaking, shop and clerical work were considered to be more respectable occupations. But they were all poorly paid, and in 1911 the dressmakers in the prestigious Ben Evans store in Swansea went on strike for better pay and conditions. Nursing and teaching, especially in the primary sector, were beginning to make an impact too as suitable caring and nurturing occupations for middle class and some working class women. On the whole, however, almost all these occupations were seen as temporary, until the women married and removed themselves from the jobs market.

Many secondary school teachers and headmistresses of girls' schools chose to remain unmarried in order to pursue a professional career in teaching. They were an impressive group, including Miss Annie Dobell (Blaenau Ffestiniog), Miss Beatrice Holme (Carmarthen) and Miss Mary Collin (Cardiff High). The latter was a committed feminist, who encouraged her girls to fulfil their true academic potential. Emily Phipps, headmistress of Swansea Central School, was an active militant suffragette and became the President of the National Federation of Women Teachers in 1915-17.

TASKS

1. Compile a list of the traditional occupations open to women pre-1914 and add to it from your own research. Which occupations were not open to them?

2. Using the sources in this section and your own research, compare and contrast the working conditions and wage levels of working women in this period.

THE IMPACT OF THE FIRST WORLD WAR

When Britain declared war on Germany and Austria on August 4, 1914, thousands of young men flocked to join the armed services. They were attracted and persuaded by the massive government propaganda campaign. Initially, however, women's experiences were different. Many employers decided to cut their costs and dismiss their female workers. This situation was overturned, however, by early 1915 as women were called upon to replace the men released for the war effort, in a practice called 'substitution'. In March 1915, women between sixteen and sixty-five were urged to register at **labour exchanges** for war work and when conscription for men was introduced in January 1916, more and more single young women decided to 'do their bit' for the war effort. For the first time the country officially declared to its female population, as it did to its men, 'Your Country Needs YOU'.

Women's war work

The militant suffragette leader, Mrs Pankhurst, said in 1915, 'If the country is to be saved women must be allowed to serve', and this was certainly the prevailing belief at the time. The first step was to fill the shoes of the men away at war by undertaking their work: delivering coal and other goods, working as 'lady postmen', taxi drivers, on the railways and on public transport. There was considerable hostility to this from many male workers, because they feared that women would steal their jobs while they were away. Also, because women were considered to be unskilled, the work itself might be downgraded and categorised as unskilled. Male workers objected initially, for example, to women working on the trams, but by March 1915 60 conductresses were employed by Cardiff Corporation Tramways and there were even some female tram drivers.

During the war women continued to work in the woollen and hosiery factories. In West Wales, the Flannel Manufacturing Company was contracted to provide 150,000 shirts in 1914 and in 1917 workshops in Blaenau Ffestiniog, Pen-y-groes and Tal-y-sarn produced 130,000 pairs of socks for the troops. Women also worked in industry: in brickyards in Dowlais, making nuts and bolts at Cwmbrân and airships and barrage balloons in Cardiff.

Women in the munitions factories

The most important factories were the munitions works, producing explosives, shells and other armaments for war. The Ministry of Munitions organized a large-scale recruitment drive to attract women into these works.

Thus the state became a major employer of women. The Woolwich Arsenal, in London, employed around 80,000 people, a high percentage of them were women. Many of these lived in hostels nearby, which were run on almost military lines. The upper class Welshwoman, Beatrice Picton Turberville from Ewenni, was in charge of 3,000 women in one of these hostels. The women began working in the small arms factory, then moved to heavy arms, crane driving and danger work, working with explosives such as TNT. Around two workers a week died, or were killed, in the danger workshops. Exposure to TNT turned skins and hair yellow and these women became known as 'canaries'. However, the women tried to enliven their work environment. Each workshop had its own fashion statement – with different coloured ribbons and the first crèche in Wales and England was opened at Woolwich Arsenal.

Similar factories were opened in Wales: making shells in Cardiff, Llanelli, Newport, Uskside, Porthmadog and Wrexham and explosives at the huge factories in Queensferry and Pembre, which was the largest and employed 11,000 men and women. Around 70-80% of these workforces were women. At Pembre the conditions were dreadful, with the girls in rags and rats everywhere, but other factories had canteens, washrooms, and even hockey and football teams for their workers. Women's work was classified as unskilled or semi-skilled, and thus they were paid less than the men. At Queensferry 12,778 accidents, including acid burns, eye injuries and skin infections, were reported and there were four deaths.

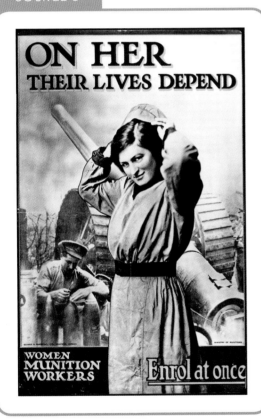

A recruitment poster for the munitions factories

The girls here are very rough, so are the conditions. ... The ether in the cordite affects the girls. It gives some headaches, hysteria, and sometimes fits. ... On a heavy windless day we sometimes have 30 girls overcome by the fumes

The testimony of Miss G. M. West, a munitions policewoman in a TNT and cordite factory in south Wales

The funeral procession of a munitions worker, Swansea 1917

TASK

Study Sources 8-10 and the other information in this section. How would women have viewed work in munitions factories during the First World War?

Women on the land

In contrast, the government tried to recruit women to help on the land, initially voluntarily and then, in 1917, through the Women's Land Army (WLA) and the Forestry Corps, by emphasising the healthy nature of the work. In fact, the work was very physically demanding, as they were called upon to plough, chop down timber, dig trenches, cut thistles etc for a meagre wage. They were often faced with the open hostility of the farmers, who felt they were totally unsuited to agricultural work. At its peak in 1918, there were 16,000 women in the Land Army and their contribution proved invaluable in keeping 'the wolf from the door', as Britain was close to starvation and had to introduce rationing.

SOURCE 11

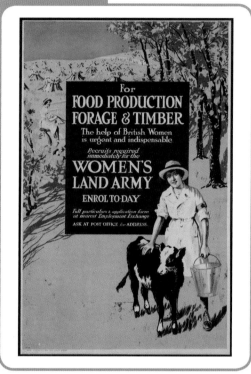

For
FOOD PRODUCTION
FORAGE & TIMBER
The help of British Women
is urgent and indispensable

Recruits required
immediately for the
WOMEN'S
LAND ARMY
ENROL TO-DAY

Full particulars & application form
at nearest Employment Exchange
ASK AT POST OFFICE for ADDRESS.

Women's Land Army recruitment poster

SOURCE 12

Many of us were Cockneys who didn't know wheat from barley, and we were of all sorts – housemaids, schoolmistresses, singers, painters, ... factory packers, ... and shop assistants.

... The pay is not good. A well-paid labourer makes £1 a week ... Women working on the land must remember that they have to be careful not to lower the wages for the men who have gone to fight. They must insist on that £1 a week. ...

The amazing thing ... was the adaptability of women. ... who would have imagined that delicately-nurtured, highly-educated women could have undertaken the work of farm labourers

The testimony of a member of the Women's Defence Relief Corps, precursor of the WLA, in The Lady: Journal for Gentlewomen, *16 March 1916*

SOURCE 13

Land Army women working at Gelli Cadwgan Farm, Builth, 1917

TASK

Study Sources 8-13. Compare and contrast work in munitions factories and in the Women's Land Army.

Nurses, doctors and women police

As might be expected, nurses were highly prized during the war. The Queen Alexandra's Imperial Military Nursing Service and the Territorial Nursing Service could offer the services of 3,000 trained nurses in 1914. They served in several different war zones: in Egypt, Gaza, and the sub-Arctic, under gruelling conditions. Others served in voluntary units such as the Volunteer Aid Detachments, who organized 112 detachments to staff 48 hospitals in Glamorganshire alone, and nursed 30,000 men during the war. Marjery Anwylyd Williams of Bridgend served as a VAD nurse in military hospitals in France and Brittany and was awarded the Royal Red Cross. Women doctors also served throughout the war, although, famously, when Dr Elsie Inglis went to offer her expertise to the War Office, she was told 'to go home and sit still'! She ignored the advice and established the Scottish Women's Hospitals, working in France and Serbia. Dr Mary Eppynt-Phillips of Brecon went out to Serbia to work in the Welsh Hospitals Unit there.

Under the Defence of the Realm Act (DORA) in 1914, there was a demand for women police. Eventually, in 1916, the Women's Police Service (WPS) was introduced – full-time workers with distinctive uniforms. They were sent to police munitions works, for example, at Pembre, Inspector Guthrie survived three explosions and was commended for her work. Through the WPS a long-held feminist aim had been achieved.

Red Cross Nurses and others parading through Caernarfon during the First World War

Women in the Services

Recruitment posters to attract women into the Services

The most remarkable change towards the end of the war was the establishment of women's **auxiliary services.** Traditionally women had always been viewed as life-givers, not life-takers like men; these services would ensure that they would be able to service those employed to kill behind the front line, but not do the killing themselves. Technically, therefore, the women remained civilians, but the mere fact of belonging to a service of 'national importance' and being paid by the government was considered a significant advance for women at the time.

The Women's Army Auxiliary Corps (WAAC) and the Women's Royal Naval Service (WRNS) were established in 1917 and the Women's Royal Air Force (WRAF) was formed in 1918. Two upper class Welshwomen served with distinction in these services: Violet Douglas-Pennant of Penrhyn Castle, became Commandant of the WRAF and Violet Picton-Turberville of Ewenni, a controller with WAAC. The government organized a strong recruitment campaign and by 1918 there were 57,000 women serving with WAAC, 32,000 WAAFs and 3,000 WRNS, mainly in kitchens, offices and as drivers. These young, single women slept in dormitories and were drilled and disciplined by male officers. Although many thought that this would be a glamorous lifestyle, the WAACs tended to be treated as scum by the public, while WRAFs were considered 'nicer' and WRNS regarded as 'perfect ladies'. As the WRAFs were not allowed to fly aeroplanes themselves they were referred to as 'penguins'.

TASKS

1. Study Sources 8, 11 and 15. Consider which messages the government used in their recruitment campaigns.

2. Write a short essay summarising women's work during the First World War

Women's work after the war

There is considerable debate and disagreement about the impact that women's work during the First World War had on women's status as workers after that war had ended. Was it to be the dawn of a bright new age or an exceptional interlude for women? Here are some of the views of contemporaries and historians:

SOURCE 16

Women are going to come out of this inferno with broken hearts and bleeding feet, but they are coming out [of] it with a strange, new, and terrible wisdom ... Women were formerly only the mothers of men; now they have risen to the dizzy height of making machine-guns

Mary Macarthur, founder of the women's trade union, the Women's Trade Union League, in her article, 'Woman's future. Is She to Go Back to Her Pots and Pans?', Llais Llafur, 27 January 1917, front page

SOURCE 17

thousands upon thousands of women workers were dismissed, and found no work to do. ... Public opinion assumed that all women could still be supported by men, and that if they went on working it was from a sort of deliberate wickedness. ... the very same people who had been heroines and the saviours of their country a few months before were now parasites, blacklegs, and limpets.

Ray Strachey, the suffragist, in her book, The Cause, 1978

SOURCE 18

All in all ... in 1918 ... [women] were thanked for their services to the nation ... and expected to disappear quietly back 'into the home'.

Historian, Deirdre Beddoe in her article 'Women between the Wars' in 1988

SOURCE 19

many women's self image and confidence had increased, and this could not be taken away from them.

Historian, Gill Thomas in her book Life on All Fronts: Women in the First World War, 1989, page 45

TASK

Study Sources 16-19. Would you say that these opinions agree with, or contradict, one another?

Certainly, after the war, ex-servicemen expected to be able to return to their former jobs as they had left them in 1914. This was enforced through the 1919 Restoration of Pre-war Practices Act. Married women, in particular, were expected to retreat into their homes to nurture their families and to release their jobs. To this effect a marriage bar preventing married women from working was introduced in the professions – for teachers, nurses and civil servants.

Single women, of whom there would be many now because of the horrific war losses, were often treated shabbily. The government offered **munitionettes** two weeks' pay and a free train journey home. By 1920 the services had all been disbanded and there were no women police in Wales. Women did receive out-of-work donations for 13 weeks, but after that they had to accept any work offered them or forfeit their payments. In these circumstances, thousands of working class girls were forced back into domestic service or laundry work, although this occupation had become extremely unpopular. In Wales in 1921 44.5% of women in work were in domestic and similar services, and by 1931 this had increased to 47.7%. Many courses were organized to prepare young girls to enter such 'situations'. Wages now ranged between 8 shillings (40p) and 15 shillings (75p) a week and although conditions had improved a little, in essence domestic service was still a very low paid, low status job.

SOURCE 20

Letitia Davies, housemaid 'in service' in a private house in Aberaeron, during the 1920s

SOURCE 21

Dosbarth coginio: dysgu bod yn forwynion – tua 1921

Cookery class in Fourcrosses, Pwllheli, 1921

SOURCE 22

I was starved to death there. She [my employer] locked everything up and gave me 3 lumps of sugar for one day and I had a small pat of margarine ... and for my dinner *every day* I had half a bag of potato crisps for 3 weeks

Oral testimony of Mrs E.D., Rhondda, 1983

The tinplate and woollen industries continued to employ women after the war but declined dramatically during the Great Depression of the late 20s and 30s. However, during these decades light industry flourished in the Midlands and south-east England and such work was considered especially suited to women. 13 new factories eventually opened on the Treforest Trading Estate in 1937-8, and the Polykoff clothing factory in the Rhondda in 1939. In Flintshire in the north-east the Courtaulds rayon factory, established in 1934, employed many women. Office jobs, as typists and secretaries, became increasingly popular and was identified as 'women's work'. The number of female shop workers doubled in this period; in 1935 it constituted the largest category of insured employed females in Wales.

The Sex Disqualification (Removal) Act of 1919 was intended to open up the professions: law, accountancy and engineering, for example, for women, but once more the marriage bar proved a stumbling block.

SOURCE 23

As Lady Rhondda, the former suffragette, wrote on 26 May 1922 in *Time and Tide*, 'This Act means nothing, we have been hoaxed'.

Some married teachers and nurses kept their marriages secret for years in order to pursue their careers. In 1919, through the Nursing Registration Act, nurses became professional workers. Nursing had an all-female workforce at this time and was extremely popular with middle-class and upper-working-class girls. Education also provided a means of escape and a career, especially for those who remained single. In 1921 the Burnham

salaries scale was introduced in primary schools, with women teachers to be paid four fifths of their male colleagues' salaries, for the same work. This led to the saying that there was 'No pay for Friday' for female teachers. Very many single qualified teachers and nurses had to leave Wales during the depression to seek work in the schools and hospitals of London, Liverpool and other large English cities.

SOURCE 24

women have contributed to their own subservient positions in hospitals, reinforcing the ... segregation of (male) doctors and (female) nurses.

... By 1927, the [hospital] Matron was earning £140 per annum [year] in comparison to the house surgeon ... on around £200 per annum (Jones 1984 p125).

O.V.Jones, 1984, *The Progress of Medicine. A History of the Caernarfon and Anglesey Infirmary 1809-1948*, Dyfed: Gomer Press

From Nurse Training in Caernarfon and Anglesey Hospital 1937-1949 *by Katherine A. Williams*

SOURCE 25

in a society where the male was dominant, and traditionally the family's bread-winner, a woman with money in her pocket, and the right to spend it as she wished, stood apart from the rest.

Author Gareth Alban Davies in 'The Fur Coat', Planet 102, on women in the Rhondda during the 1930s

TASKS

1. Study Sources 20-25 and the other information in this section. How would you sum up the gains and losses for women in their work experiences during the interwar period?

2. How were the experiences of single and married women different?

THE IMPACT OF THE SECOND WORLD WAR

Once more, Britain was mobilised for war in 1939. This time the war front was on the home front itself, and women were expected to cope with rationing, evacuations, blackouts and great anxieties for their loved ones. There was one other vital difference in women's experiences this time: Britain was the first country in

Europe to introduce conscription for women. All 19-40 year olds were categorised as 'mobile' or 'immobile' and they had to register for work of 'national importance' anywhere in Britain, unless they had children under 14, were too old or already in essential employment. Employers were compelled through the Essential Work

Order (March 1941), to take them on. In December 1941 the National Service (No. 2) Act brought in conscription for single 20-30 year olds, now they were compelled to work in industry or the services. In 1942-43 married women were called upon too and in 1944 the age of registration was raised to 50. Those who refused to register were called conscientious objectors (or conshis). Pegi Lloyd Williams of Blaenau Ffestiniog recalled how she was hauled before a military tribunal for refusing to register and how she was treated with great contempt by the female officers.

At the beginning of the war, once more, women substituted (for less pay usually) as telephonists, ambulance drivers, truckers and conductresses for the men who were away at war. Many others were drawn through propaganda and conscription into the **auxiliary services**, as they had been at the end of the First World War. In many cases women performed the usual traditional roles within these services as clerks, domestics, cooks etc, but many were also employed in much more skilled and technical jobs, deciphering codes or working with radar. The status of the Auxiliary Territorial Service (ATS) was low and the women who joined it considered rather 'common'. They had to march and parade like soldiers and they earned around £1 a week. Members of the Women's Royal Naval Service (WRNS, popularly called WRENS) had a superior image, whilst the Women's Auxiliary Air Force (WAAFS) were considered glamorous. Many of these developed skills as welders, flight mechanics and **meteorologists**.

SOURCE 26

Recruitment poster for the ATS

SOURCE 27

I can tell you all about the A.T.S. ... I've made lots of friends. In my unit only 40 girls out of 190 do any housework. The rest of us do clerical work ...

The food is very good and we get lots of amusement – for instance, we have a dance every week.

The men accept us now as equals and respect us for doing the technical jobs efficiently.

Private P. Barnikel in the North Wales Chronicle *19 December, 1941, page 2*

SOURCE 28

Marjorie Edmunds from Llanelli, a WAAF engineer who worked on Spitfire and Anson Aircraft, reclining on the nose of an aeroplane

SOURCE 29

Molly Stevens (née Perry) a petty officer in the WRNS in her official uniform, Portsmouth, 1943

Women were called upon to work in industry too. In Llanberis and Caernarfon 3,000 workers, mostly women, worked for the North East Aircraft Company, making parts for bombers; in Broughton 6,000 workers, about half of them women made Wellington bombers and in Waunarlwydd, near Swansea 2,000 workers made sheet and strip aluminium for aircraft. However the most important industry, once again, was the munitions industry. Huge factories were established at Bridgend (employing 35,000 at its peak with 70% of them women), Hirwaun, Pontypool, Marchwiel, Pembre and other areas. It was dangerous work. The Bridgend works was called 'the Suicide Club' and about 25 women were killed there. If they worked with TNT they would be called canaries. It turned blonde hair green, black hair orange and brown hair yellow.

Women travelled by train from all over south Wales to work the three shifts that kept the factories going day and night. But wages were comparatively good. A munitions worker could earn from £2. 15s (£2.75) to £4.10s (£4.50) a week, which was higher than that paid to an underground miner. As a result there was considerable resentment, especially as this was such an unusual situation in Wales. Many miners feared that the world had been turned upside down. Furthermore, working condition were better in the factories than in the mines, with canteens as well as entertainment in organized dances and concerts. However it is important to remember that, within the factories and the services, men doing the same work as women were paid higher wages and all attempts at changing this by women

MPs were unsuccessful. Also women often found that they had two jobs to fulfil – in the war effort and as housewives in their own homes. For many, they shouldered a double burden during the war.

Recruitment poster 'Where is Mrs Jones Going?' calling upon married women to join the munitions workers

I thought I was doing a man's work but I never thought I was taking a man's job. It was just the war.

The oral testimony of Mrs Jones (born in Gwynedd in 1921), who worked in an aeroplane factory

he [William Paynter] said that ... miners came home after six days' hard grind at the coal-face with less money in their pay packets than a girl of 18 working in a munitions factory.

William Paynter, miners' agent at a Communist-organized rally at Aberdare in March 1942, as reported in the Aberdare Leader *on 4 April 1942*

Once more too, the Women's Land Army played its part in the war effort. By 1943, there were 80,000 members, 1,000 of them rat catchers. Farmers had to pay them £1 2s 6d (£1.12½) a week but were very sceptical about women's ability to drive tractors and work on the land. Most of the women proved their worth, as did the 6,000 Timber Jills who worked for the Timber Corps, sawing wood for telegraph poles and pit props.

SOURCE 33

Members of the Timber Corps, Gunley Hall, Welshpool, October 1942

SOURCE 34

"Now, Miss Fforbes-Wattson, have you had any experience of agricultural work?"

A cartoon poking fun at an upper class 'town girl' called up to the Women's Land Army

SOURCE 35

Janet Ivy Griffiths, Abersoch in the War Ag Centre, Chwilog, Caernarvonshire, c.1945

TASK

Write a short newspaper article about work in the Women's Land Army during the war. Sources 33-35 should be included.

During the war, nurses were crucial in the war effort and many Welsh women served in hospitals for wounded soldiers throughout Wales and England. Queen Alexandra Nurses sailed with the forces to war areas. Margaret Griffiths of Pontllan-fraith travelled to Sierra Leone and Gambia and Sister Megan Morris of Fochriw sailed with the Normandy Landing crafts in June 1944. She and her fellow nurses slept in trenches and worked as theatre sisters in the field, sometimes for over 25 hours non-stop. Although police ranks had been closed to women after the First World War, the Women's Auxiliary Police Force (WAPC) was created during the Second World War and by 1942-43 policewomen had been appointed, mostly as office workers, in every Welsh county.

All in all therefore, the war brought far more women into full-time, paid work. In Wales the percentage rise in insured female workers was 134% (in Wales and England it was 30%). In 1939, 94,000 women worked in Wales; by 1945 the figure was 204,000.

SOURCE 36

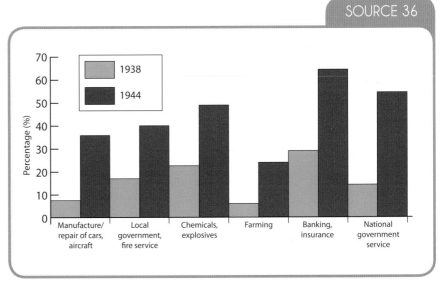

A bar chart illustrating the number of workers who were women in Britain in 1938 and 1944

After the war

Expectations that conditions would remain the same for women as they had during the war, as far as work was concerned, were not as great as after the First World War. After all the government had emphasised in all its propaganda campaigns that women's war work would only be 'for the duration'. In fact, many wives and mothers were glad to return to doing one job instead of two. Others looked forward to settling down and there was a marriage, and a baby, boom in the post-war era.

However, many other women had had a taste of financial independence and social freedom during the war years; their horizons had been widened and they felt much more assertive and self-confident. They resented being thrown aside once more and began to question why that should be the case. Indeed, the Second World War would prove to be a significant changing point in the story of women's experiences in the workplace.

SOURCE 37

And after it was over you had to learn again
To be just wives and mothers when you'd done the work of men ...

And you never thought to question
You just went on with your lives
'Cause all they taught you who to be
Was mothers, daughters, wives.

A popular song, written by Judy Small in 1982, about her mother's experience after the Second World War

SOURCE 38

In 1945, her praises no longer sung, her skills no longer needed, the sensible housewife was expected to down tools and return to her knitting.

Historian Angela Holdsworth, in Out of the Doll's House, *1988*

TASK

How useful are Source 37 and 38 to historians studying women's work after the Second World War?

This section provides guidance on how to answer question 1(a) from Units 1 and 2. It is a source comprehension question, which is worth 2 marks.

Question 1(a) – comprehension of a visual source

What does Source A show you about women's work during the First World War?

[2 marks]

SOURCE A

Women crane workers in a shell factory during the First World War

Tips on how to answer

This is an inference question involving the comprehension of a visual source.

- You are being asked to **look into the picture** and **pick out** relevant details.

- You must also make use of the **statement next to the source**, which is intended to provide you with additional information.

- You must **only comment on what you can see** in the picture and what is written next to the source. Do not bring in additional factual knowledge as this will not score you marks.

- To obtain maximum marks you will need to **pick out at least two relevant points** that are well developed and supported.

The candidate has merely copied the statement written below the source. This is not a developed answer. It would get one mark for one observation.

The candidate has made a number of valid observations based upon the source and caption. This is a developed answer worthy of 2 marks. The candidate correctly infers that work was dangerous for women and that they had taken the place of fighting men. However, this would not be credited.

What does Source B show you about women's work during the First World War?

[2 marks]

A female worker turning the copper band of a high explosive shell during the First World War

60

HOW DID EMPLOYMENT OPPORTUNITIES FOR WOMEN IN WALES AND ENGLAND CHANGE AFTER THE SECOND WORLD WAR?

Introduction

SOURCE 1

A cartoon demonstrating 1960s attitudes towards educating girls and boys

TASK

What does this cartoon tell us about attitudes towards the education of girls and boys in the post-war period?

CHANGES IN EDUCATION

Before 1944 few children had access to secondary education. Most pupils attended elementary schools from the age of five up to the school leaving age of 14. To gain entry into secondary education, in grammar schools, pupils had to pay fees or pass 'the scholarship'. In urban areas, such as Llanelli, Gowerton, Carmarthen and Aberdare, there would be separate girls' and boys' grammar schools, but the emphasis in both would have been primarily on academic subjects.

The impact of increased opportunities in secondary and higher education

The 1942 Beveridge Report had identified 'Ignorance' as one of the 'Five Evil Giants' (see Chapter 2) that needed to be eliminated in the post war period. This was to be achieved through the Education Act of 1944, which provided free secondary education for all, up to the compulsory age of 15. This Act transformed the educational opportunities open to girls and the working classes in particular. In this period too the **marriage bar,** which compelled women to resign when they married, was abolished.

The 1944 Act introduced a three-tiered system of secondary education. The Grammar Schools, with their strong focus on literature, science, mathematics and the classics (Latin and Greek), were intended for the more academic. To enter the grammar schools pupils had to pass the **11+ examination** (also called the scholarship). Only 25% of children in Wales and England passed it during this period. There is evidence to suggest that girls had to score higher marks than boys in this examination in order to win a place in a grammar school. Facilities in girls' grammar schools were sometimes inferior to those of boys' grammar schools, especially in the provision of science laboratories.

SOURCE 2

It was an important day ... [there was] a fear of failing. You were very conscious then that your future, although you were only young, ten / eleven ... depended upon which school you went to.

The oral testimony of Margaret Evans, Llangefni, explaining the significance of 'scholarship day', c.1950

SOURCE 3

Sixth form Chemistry class at Ardwyn Grammar School, Aberystwyth in the 1950s. Note the only two female students among a sea of male students

SOURCE 4

Sixth form science lesson at Brynhyfryd Secondary School, Rhuthun, around 1955. Note the lack of laboratory facilities

SOURCE 5

the grammar schools ... were a world of gowned mistresses, prefects, ... rules, school uniforms – box-pleated gymslips, ... and school hats, hockey, lacrosse and netball and strict discipline, enforced by detention and 'lines'.

Historian, Deirdre Beddoe, based upon her own experiences as a pupil at Barry Girls Grammar School in the 1950s

The second tier was the Secondary Technical Schools, designed to train pupils in mechanical and scientific subjects. However, few of these were established. The majority of pupils (around 75%), therefore, attended Secondary Modern Schools, which were more vocational in focus and based on training in practical skills. Thus girls' education was centred on domestic subjects – cooking and needlework – and on typing and commerce (business), to prepare them for office work. They were educated for what was considered to be their main function in life, which was to be effective wives and mothers. The Crowther Education Report of 1959 promoted this idea further.

The Newsom Education Report of 1963 reaffirmed the attitudes of the Crowther Report and even advised that girl pupils should practise the skill of running a home in a flat provided by the school.

Jane Salisbury, writing of her secondary school experiences in the 1960s, depicts how girls and boys were prepared for narrow gender roles and how certain curriculum areas were highly gendered. She describes what was a domestic apprenticeship for girls and the specialist teaching space for Home Economics lessons:

SOURCE 7

They took place in what was a modern open plan fitted kitchen. It twinkled with new white electric cookers and gleaming double drainer sink units. ... A little flat led off the kitchen ... where we were taught how to create a 'dining ambience' [atmosphere] (full cutlery, candles and napkins). ... We accepted the learned skills as a valuable contribution to our futures as wives and mothers. Boys did woodwork and never crossed the threshold of the kitchen.

The testimony of Jane Salisbury, (born Barry, 1955) and a pupil at St Cadoc's Roman Catholic Secondary Modern School, describing the cookery lessons

SOURCE 8

I remember I was given a choice ... cookery, Latin or woodwork for the boys – that was the choice in form three. So, I wanted to go and do cookery ... I didn't want to do Latin and I remember the headmaster saying to me, 'You can learn how to cook at home girl, go and do Latin'.

The oral testimony of Mererid James, who attended the grammar stream at Machynlleth (bilateral) Secondary School, c. 1958

In rural areas of Wales, **bilateral schools** were created with two separate streams – grammar school and secondary modern pupils. This was the case at Aberaeron, Lampeter, and Tregaron in Ceredigion. These streams were usually kept separate and the grammar stream was treated as the most prestigious.

Dramatic changes took place from the late 1960s onwards regarding education in general and in girls' participation in it. Comprehensive schools, where all the pupils from the same neighbourhood would attend the same school, irrespective of their individual abilities and aptitudes, were created and pupils weren't segregated in most aspects of the curriculum according to gender (female/male) or academic abilities. In 1965, 15% of the secondary pupils in Wales attended comprehensive schools; by 1985 the percentage had risen to 99%. At the beginning of the 1970s the school leaving age was raised to 16. However mathematics, physics and chemistry, the 'difficult' sciences, were still viewed primarily as boys' subjects and biology, languages and the arts considered more suitable for girls. The Sex Discrimination Act of 1975 made it illegal to offer separate subjects for boys and girls. Now, boys could join in cookery or home economics classes and girls were actively encouraged to take up the sciences. In 1984 Women in Science and Engineering was set up, but even in 1991, of the 200 school leavers in Wales who went on to study engineering, only 4% were female.

In 1988 the old 'O' Level examinations were abandoned and were replaced by General Certificate of Secondary Education (GCSE) examinations for 16+ pupils. This was felt to be a fairer system. It was especially attractive to girls because coursework became an important aspect of these examinations, and girls responded well to this form of assessment. By 1991 girls in Wales were gaining higher success rates than boys in 46 (out of 60) GCSE subjects. The introduction of a national curriculum in the 1988 Education Act ensured that girls and boys would be taught the same subjects at all times.

TASK

List the different types of secondary education systems that were available between c.1945 and the 1970s and note the main characteristics of each one.

After their school years many of the secondary modern sector students progressed to further education colleges to learn vocational subjects such as typing, shorthand and hairdressing. These experiences allowed young women to seek employment as secretaries, typists and hairdressers, which were very gendered occupations, in offices and salons.

SOURCE 9

Young women learning shorthand at a college of further education in the 1960s

In rural areas young farmers were encouraged to attend further education courses in centres such as Llysfasi, Denbighshire and Felin-fach, Cardiganshire. At the Farmers' Education Centre in Felin-fach the courses were highly gendered in the 1950s and 60s, with men studying mechanics and women on rural domestic economy courses.

SOURCE 10

Young farmers studying in the 'laboratory' at the Farmers' Education Centre, Felin-fach in the 1950s

SOURCE 11

Young women farmers following a course in 'Rural Domestic Economy' at the Farmers' Education Centre, Felin-fach, in the 1960s

The most popular vocations for women who had succeeded in the educational system in the post-war period, however, were still nursing and teaching. Nursing Colleges, which combined academic lectures and practical experiences, flourished. Iona Davies of Solfach trained in Haverfordwest General Hospital in the 1950s and stayed in the Nurses' Home:

[We] started at half past seven in the morning, then on the wards until nine and then ... to school for Anatomy and Physiology ... until half past four. ... We lived in [the nurses' home] in Haverfordwest ... there were staunch rules at that time. You had to be in by ten every night ... (If you broke the rules) I think you had to do a stint on night duty. That's probably why I was such a night owl!

The oral testimony of Iona Davies, Solfach

You had your dress ... your lodging ... and food. I think ... in the first year we earned about £8 10s. [£8.50] a month. ... You just accepted it, ... and you were glad to be in work.

The oral testimony of Rhian Llwyd Wynne Jones, Cerrigydrudion, who trained to be a nurse in Rossett, Wrexham, in the early 1960s

Since the 1940s medical schools had opened their doors to women students; with a ratio of a minimum of one female student to every five males.

Young women aspiring to be primary school teachers flocked to the teacher training colleges in the Normal and St Mary's, Bangor, Wrexham, Swansea, Barry and Cyncoed, Cardiff. In 1957, Trinity College, Carmarthen, admitted girls for the first time and within a decade there were more female than male students. One female student claimed that the college had 'become a gentler place'. Stormy meetings were held over proposals to impose different standards for the female students, such as an earlier time for being in their halls of residence at night. The strict rules that governed the female students' lives in their halls of residence were a constant irritant in both training colleges and universities from the 1950s to the 1980s.

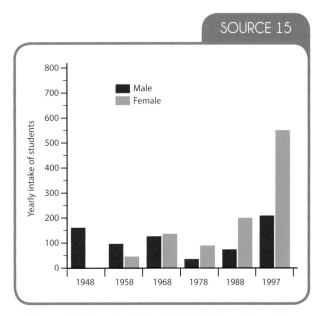

The yearly intake of students at Trinity College, Carmarthen, showing the numbers of male and female students

Barry Training College students with local MP Dorothy Rees, visiting the House of Commons; c. 1950

More and more young women were entering higher education. In British Universities in the 1970s only 30% of the undergraduates were female, but by the late-90s they outnumbered male undergraduates. Once more, however, many of the female graduates qualified as teachers, primarily in the secondary sector. Unfortunately, there was a glut of qualified primary and secondary teachers from the Welsh colleges and they had to seek work in England, especially in cities such as Liverpool, Birmingham and London. Indeed, in the 1960s 70% of London teachers were Welsh.

Aberdare Hall ... you were invited every now and then to sit with them [the staff at the top table] – you weren't allowed to raise your knife and fork until she [the warden] raised her knife and fork! ... On Sundays you were allowed to invite friends, boys in for tea. ... And you had to be in by ten every night ... We had to wear gowns to go to lectures then ...

The oral testimony of Margarette Hughes, from Whitland, who studied Philosophy at Cardiff University in the 1960s and who lived in the women's hostel at Aberdare Hall

SOURCE 17

I was born in 1942, I passed the scholarship and ... went to ... Barry Girls' County Grammar School and was free. I went on to university, and was the first person in my family to do so: I was enabled to do this by the existence of student grants

Historian, Deirdre Beddoe, reflecting upon her own educational experiences, through grammar school to university in the 1950s and 60s

Young female students enjoying the facilities of a modern hostel at University College Aberystwyth in 1981

SOURCE 18

TASKS

1. Explain the statistics in Source 15 in your own words.

2. Using Sources 9-18 and other information provided, discuss how the male and female experiences of further and higher education were different.

3. Note the main features of women's experiences in further training and education in this period.

CHANGES IN WORKING OPPORTUNITIES

With the improved educational opportunities for girls and young women in the secondary, further and higher education sectors in this period, it would be natural to assume that this would be reflected in their employment opportunities and in equality in the workplace. However, was this really the case?

SOURCE 19

Certainly since the Second World War in Wales there has been substantial equality of opportunity within the school system, and increasingly in the further- and higher-education system, for both sexes. This has not been reflected in post-school equality of opportunities of employment, promotion or pay. Nor has it dramatically transformed the patterns of employment for women which characterized the twentieth century – the most popular job for women being clerical, with strong representation in the teaching and caring professions.

Historians Gareth Elwyn Jones and Gordon Wynne Roderick in their book, A History of Education in Wales, 2003

During the Second World War both single and married women had entered the workforce in great numbers and had earned better wages than had been possible previously. Indeed, as we have seen (Chapter 4), many women had enjoyed a taste of financial independence and social freedom and were not prepared to return to unpaid work in the home as housewives. The **marriage bar** in teaching, the civil service and other professions, was lifted in this period too and the pattern changed dramatically. Married women tended to work until their first child was born now, and then to return to paid work, often part-time, once the children had entered full-time education. This meant that women were regarded as fleeting figures, dropping in and out of the labour market to suit their own circumstances. The jobs available to women, outside the professions, were often low or semi-skilled ones, which were poorly paid and of low status. Women were definitely not seen or treated as breadwinners, who should earn a 'family wage', even when they were single parents. Their pay was seen as an extra bonus, a second income, to supplement the main (male) breadwinner's pay packet and used for holidays, the children's education and new household gadgets, such as fridges and food processors. Some women were not willing to accept this situation and the fight for equal pay for equal work and for fair conditions and no discrimination in the workplace is one of the main features of this post-war period (Chapter 9).

Work in light industry

As wartime factories closed, new companies, often branches of large UK or overseas firms, opened light industry factories. They realised that there was a huge reservoir of female labour available in Wales, and there was a belief that women were naturally good at the fiddly, mindless, repetitive tasks required in light industry. Such work was considered unsuitable for male heavy industry workers. Another attraction was that few women were members of trade unions and the new companies were looking for a docile and **compliant** female workforce.

SOURCE 21

A cartoon by Viv Quillin illustrating male attitudes towards working women (1984)

Large industrial estates were developed from the former Royal Ordnance Munitions factories at Bridgend, Hirwaun and Marchwiel (Wrexham) and many women workers moved from Bridgend to the Metal Box factory in Briton Ferry. By 1970 3,500 people, a high percentage of them women, worked at this factory. In Llandudno Junction the former aircraft components factory was transformed by Hotpoint into a washing machine factory, employing 2,000 workers. Likewise, in 1948, Hoover built an Art Deco factory in Pentre-bach, Merthyr Tydfil, to produce washing machines, and although initially men were the main workers on the production line itself, women were also key workers there.

SOURCE 20

A cartoon by Leslie Illingworth illustrating the demand for equal pay in the post-war period

Women checking Corgi model cars at the Mettoy factory, Swansea, 1982

In 1981 there was a dispute regarding discrimination against the women workers in this factory, as the men attempted to force their women co-workers off a redundancy scheme. The Community Video Workshop at Chapter, Cardiff, made a video called *Political Annie's Off Again*, based upon this dispute.

Car assembly plants were a major employer of women too, as at Dagenham in the West Midlands, where the famous strike by the women machinists, calling for equal pay for their skilled work, took place in 1968 (Chapter 6). In Caernarfon, women worked at the Ferodo car component plant, opened in 1962, and when Ford set up an engine plant in Bridgend in 1980, women formed a significant proportion of the workforce. On the Hirwaun industrial estate televisions were assembled, and later the Japanese companies, including Sony of Bridgend, were established, employing women to make parts for the computer industry. They took their place on the assembly lines at toy factories such as Lines Brothers, Merthyr Tydfil (1951 onwards), and Mettoy in

Swansea, which opened in 1982. Among the host of other factories employing women were the Bear Brand nylon stocking factory in Corwen and the Revlon makeup factory in Maesteg, whilst in the Rhondda 25 new factories opened between 1945 and 1955, making such things as Christmas decorations, tape decks, telephone dials and bicycles. In the 1960s 85% of the workforce in the clothing factories were skilled female machinists but only 15% of the managers were women.

Although conditions and pay were not ideal in such factories, many of them did offer medical facilities and canteens, and the women particularly enjoyed the social life associated with works' dos, parties and trips. Some factories even organized their own beauty competitions.

Pat Owen, chosen as Miss AEI-Hotpoint, Llandudno Junction in 1961

One hidden source of light industry in the post-war era was the number of home workers, estimated at over one million in the UK, who assembled and packaged retail items, sold in the major UK chains, in their own homes. The work was often fiddly, labour intensive and skilled (e.g. making Christmas crackers). Many worked unsociable hours packing goods for overnight despatch to supermarkets, for well under the minimum wage. This invisible workforce consisted mainly of women, often from ethnic minorities.

TASK

What is light industry? Give examples from the sources and the text above. Why were women considered particularly suited to such jobs? What were the disadvantages for women?

The service industries

After the war the sector that made the greatest impact on women's employment was the service sector. This included jobs in offices, banking, supermarkets, tourism, catering and hairdressing. Indeed, 40% of Welsh women workers were in the service industries in the 1960s and 70s. On the whole, however, sexual stereotyping of jobs was still strong, with cooking, cleaning and looking after people being important elements of most of the services noted.

Although the traditional domestic servant disappeared during the Second World War, domestic work itself did not disappear. It became professionalised during the post-war period, as women worked as cleaners and cooks in offices, hospitals, factories and schools and as home-helps and cleaners in private homes. As before, these jobs were considered to be of low status and were poorly paid. When black migrant workers arrived in Britain in the 1950s and 60s, they were often forced into these menial occupations.

SOURCE 24

I resented it badly, very badly … In our house [in Jamaica] we had people who came in to do that kind of work for us, and they were like part of our family. … These people treated you like muck. I sometimes want to cry really when I think about it.

Amanda Murphy, an immigrant from Jamaica, on scrubbing floors in Britain in the 1960s

In 1972 the night-cleaners of London went on strike to seek better wages and the right to belong to a union. Eventually they won their case for a wage of £16.50 a week and no victimisation.

There was a huge increase in demand for secretaries, shorthand typists, **comptometers** and office clerks, for example in the administration of the National Health Service from 1948 onwards and in local government. Much of this work was in the public sector, with such centres as the Royal Mint, Llantrisant, which opened in 1968, and the DVLA (formerly the DVLC) in Swansea, opened in 1965 and which employed many women among its 4,000 workforce. The personal secretary became a highly influential, though still subservient, figure.

SOURCE 25

Many women's jobs involve actually seeing to the personal needs of male bosses, such as taking his suit to the cleaners … buying presents for his wife – [being] the 'office wife'

Historian Victoria Winckler in her article about women in post-war Wales

In the field of tourism, the hotel and café trade flourished and holiday camps such as Butlin's, opened in Pwllheli in 1947, and in Barry in 1966, were very popular. Again, women found themselves in great demand as cleaners, office workers and some as entertainers. Marian Kneale recalls being a Redcoat entertainer, earning £6 a week with board and lodging, at Butlin's camp, Barry in 1970.

As farms became mechanised and there was less demand for farmers' wives to do outside work, many of them supplemented the farm income by offering 'Bed and Breakfast' to travelling tourists. Indeed, farmers' wives became strong advocates and promoters of farm tourism, developing self-catering holidays and other attractions, which contributed substantially to their incomes.

Supermarkets and large department stores, which proliferated in town centres from the 1950s onwards, also provided employment opportunities for women as check-out operators, cashiers and stores workers.

During the period up to 1980, the number of women in the workforce in Wales was increasing by an average of over 2% a year, as 94,000 women entered the workforce after 1965. The vast majority of these were in the service sector.

Changes in Women's Employment in Services 1965-1981

	Changes in Employment			
	1965-74		1974-81	
	Numbers	%	Numbers	%
Transport & Communication	+1,000	+12%	0	0
Distribution	−6,000	−10%	0	0
Insurance, Banking & Finance	+3,000	+30%	+4,000	+29%
Professional and Scientific Services	+23,000	+29%	+22,000	+22%
Miscellaneous services	+11,000	+25%	+14,000	+25%
Public Administration & Defence	+7,000	+25%	+4,000	+15%
Total Service Employment	+39,000	+17.3%	+43,000	+16.2%

Department of Employment Gazette *1976; Census of Employment 1981*

1. Explain the statistics in Source 26 in your own words.

2. What is the service industry? Give examples from the sources and text above. What status did most women have in these industries?

Female economic activity rates increased significantly during this period. In Wales the rates had been: 23.6% of women as registered workers in 1911; 21% in 1931; 24.9% in 1951 and 36.07% in 1971, with a further increase during the 70s as the table in Source 27 shows.

Women as a percentage of registered workers, June 1977

Penarth	60%	Machynlleth	40%
Treorchy	57%	Merthyr Tydfil	40%
Swansea	47%	Cardiff	43%
Llandudno	54%	Porthmadog	46%
Haverfordwest	45%	Wrexham	41%

From the Digest of Welsh Statistics *1981*

It would seem therefore, that by 1980 the future for women's employment opportunities in Wales was quite bright. But these statistics must be seen against a background of great losses in male employment as the heavy industries (steel and coal) closed. And there were several other worrying trends. More and more women were being forced into part-time jobs, for which they earned substantially lower wages and brought insecurity in terms of paid holidays and maternity rights. It was hard to be a breadwinner on part-time wages.

Indeed, it is possible to question whether there had been a fundamental shift in the nature of women's work in this period after all, and whether the gender stereotyping of jobs had actually been challenged in any way.

TASK

Discuss the changing working opportunities for women after the Second World War.

Examination practice

This section provides guidance on how to answer question 1(d) from Units 1 and 2. It involves the analysis and evaluation of the utility of a source and is worth six marks.

Question 1(d) – the analysis and evaluation of the utility of a source

How useful is Source A to the historian studying working opportunities for women in Wales in the twenty first century?

[6 marks]

SOURCE A

Key findings include:

- A survey of 50 top private companies in Wales found only two female chief executives (or equivalent head position).
- Only 9% of council leaders in Wales are women. Only 27% of councillors in Wales are women.
- Only 32% of secondary school head teachers in Wales are women, despite 75% of the workforce across primary and secondary schools being women.
- Only 23% of local authority chief executives in Wales are women, despite 72% of all local authority staff being women.

From 'Who runs Wales?', an official report of employment opportunities carried out by the Equality and Human Rights Commission, published in 2012

Tips on how to answer

This question will usually involve the analysis and evaluation of a primary source.

- In your answer you will need to **evaluate the usefulness** of this primary source in terms of its content, its origins and its purpose. Some schools find it useful to use memory aids to help structure answers. One of these involves looking at three aspects of the source in question:

Content	Origin	Purpose
What does the source say?	Who said it? When did they say it?	Why was it said? Who was it said to and why? Is it biased?

- You should aim to write about **two to three sentences** about the content of the source, putting the information into your own words and **supporting** it with your own knowledge of the topic.

- You should then comment upon the **author** of the source, noting **when** the source was written and **under what circumstances.**

- You should consider **why** the source was written and **whether** or not this makes the source biased. Remember that a **biased** source can still be very useful to the historian and do not just dismiss it.

- To obtain **maximum marks** your answer must contain **reasoned comments** upon each of the **three** elements. If you only write about the content of the source **do not expect** to get more than half marks.

Response by candidate one

This source comes from the 'Equality and Human Rights Commission'. It says that <u>women do not get the top jobs in Wales even though most women work in the council, schools or local authorities</u>. This source is very useful to historians because it was carried out by the <u>Equal Opportunities Commission and so will give an accurate picture of women in work.</u>

The candidate begins to discuss content but there is little development. There is no own knowledge. The candidate merely paraphrases the attribution and offers nothing else. This is a simplistic answer and scores 3 out of 6 marks.

Response by candidate two

Source A is very useful to an historian because it is an <u>official report from an organisation to which Parliament has given authority to promote equality and point out unfair practice.</u> Therefore what it says should be accurate and fair. <u>This is obviously a formal inquiry into employment and it is showing that women are being discriminated against. It is trying to end gender discrimination by highlighting the unfair treatment of women in Wales</u>. It is likely that the people will have had much experience in writing reports but they may exaggerate some parts of the report to suit themselves. In this case it is meant to show discrimination against women. However, the report confirms what I know about the fact that <u>despite improved education for women they are still frustrated that the best jobs are not open to them. However, some women like Margaret Thatcher and Anita Roddick</u> have shown that some women can make it to the top. <u>Historians would find this data useful to reach a judgement on working opportunities for women, but data alone does not explain why this trend has occurred in Wales. The fact that it is the key findings and not the full report may reduce its utility.</u>

Refers to attribution

Refers to purpose of source

Uses content to demonstrate wider knowledge

A good attempt to analyse the utility of the source

The candidate demonstrates a high degree of understanding and is able to evaluate in terms of content, origin and purpose. The candidate refers to the attribution and uses some context.

The candidate does not paraphrase the content but uses it with additional information to demonstrate knowledge, although the knowledge is about Britain rather than Wales. The candidate refers to the purpose of the Source and evaluates its utility as source. The candidate has made a good attempt to analyse and evaluate the utility of the source and would be credited with the full 6 marks .

Now you have a go

SOURCE B

Funny Girls: Cartooning for Equality. Preface (p. xviii) by Shelagh Diplock, Director of the Fawcett Society 1992-98

Many young women, having grown up in a new atmosphere of equal rights, are wondering what all the fuss was about. They take for granted that they have the same capabilities and opportunities as men. They are not willing to accept unfair treatment or harassment at work, and when they become mothers, they are looking for practical support to balance work and home. They do not want to be made to feel guilty whatever they choose to do, paid work or full-time motherhood. They want to be valued as women, as mothers, as individuals.

Shelagh Diplock, writing in a pamphlet for the Fawcett Society in 2006 .
The Fawcett Society is an organization that campaigns for women's rights

Question

How useful is Source B to the historian studying changes in working opportunities for women in the twenty first century?

[6 marks]

CHAPTER 6

HOW SUCCESSFUL HAVE WOMEN BEEN IN TAKING ADVANTAGE OF NEW EMPLOYMENT OPPORTUNTIES IN WALES AND ENGLAND?

Introduction

SOURCE 1

A cartoon by Jacky Fleming reflecting upon men's attitudes to women in 'top jobs', 1995

BREAKING THROUGH THE 'GLASS CEILING'

Background

Since women's work and educational opportunities seemed to have improved substantially during the 1960s and 70s, it was expected that more able and ambitious women would be able to proceed naturally, during the following decades, into top jobs, in all kinds of employment. However such expectations have to be seen against the economic background of the period, and especially against the recession of the early 1980s. In fact, the 1980s was not a good decade for women in work.

TASK

Consider what point the cartoonist is trying to make in Source 1 about men's attitudes towards women aspiring to be appointed to top jobs in this period.

In Wales, especially, while there had been 414,000 women in work in 1979, by 1986 the figure had fallen to 377,000, and women had been effectively pushed out of the manufacturing industries. Much of the work that was available in this decade was part-time and of comparatively low status. Indeed, women were earning only 73% of the average wage of men in 1994, and in every occupation men earned more per hour than women.

Yet, many positive steps had, and have, been taken in the last forty years to try to adjust and redress the male/female work and pay imbalance. In 1970 the Equal Pay Act was passed and followed in 1975 by the Sex Discrimination Act, which banned discrimination between the sexes in employment, education and advertising and set up the Equal Opportunities Commission to monitor its application. In the same year the Employment Protection Act made it unlawful to dismiss a woman because she was pregnant and established the right to maternity leave and some maternity pay. During the next decades these acts were refined and amended to further protect women in the workplace.

Feminists, who fought for equality between the sexes, were also influential in this debate. Germaine Greer's controversial book, *The Female Eunuch,* was published in 1970. In it, under the chapter on 'Work', she listed women achievers in business, the clothing trade and television, and then set a challenge:

SOURCE 2

The onus is on women, who must not only equal men in the race for employment, but outstrip them. Such an incentive must ultimately be an advantage.

Likewise, Welsh-born acclaimed feminist, Elaine Morgan, in her book *The Descent of Woman: The Classic Study of Evolution,* published in 1972, questioned male domination of society by describing the evolution of woman as well as man. Such arguments helped to fuel the debate regarding the inequalities between men and women and challenged fundamentally the traditional views of women as incapable of, or unwilling to aspire to reach for the top.

SOURCE 3

The Descent of Woman
The Classic Study of Evolution

Elaine Morgan
Author of *The Aquatic Ape Hypothesis*

The front cover of Elaine Morgan's book

However, when women did not take that huge leap forward into the top jobs as expected in the 1980s and 1990s, people began to talk of a '**glass ceiling**' of prejudices and injustices, which denied them promotion and career success.

SOURCE 4

Women ... are dramatically excluded from all the jobs that command high salaries, power and visible decision-making ... They are denied the truly interesting jobs as well as the swank and the booty. The reason for this nationwide exclusion is clear. Men hold such jobs, have held them and intend to go on doing so.

Feminist historian Diana Souhami, in her book, A Woman's Place: The Changing Picture of Women in Britain, *1986*

Some feminists hoped that Margaret Thatcher, the first female Prime Minister of Britain (1979-1990), would provide an excellent role model in this respect. She had, after all, managed to smash the most prestigious of 'glass ceilings'. However, the opposite was true. Thatcher may have smashed the glass ceiling herself, but then she went on to reinforce it. She believed that the battle for women's rights had been won to all intents and purposes and she opposed laws that promoted equality.

1. Compare and contrast the views expressed in Sources 2 and 4. Which would you say has a positive attitude towards women's capabilities and which takes a negative attitude and tries to blame others?

2. Explain the phrase 'a glass ceiling'.

Women as business leaders

SOURCE 5

Percentage and numbers of women in top positions in business (1970s onwards)

Female workforce in managerial jobs: 20% (1980s)

Female members of British Institute of Management: 3% (1980s)

Female members of Law Society (solicitors): 20% (1980s)

Female Chief Executives of FTSE (Financial Times Stock Exchange) 100 companies: 3% (2006)

In the FTSE 100 companies 45 companies had no female member of their Board of Directors; 45 others had one member only and 10 companies had 2 members. (2000)

The Stock Exchange did not allow women to join until 1973.

Female principal local government officers: 3.5% (1995)

TASK

Would you say that these statistics and percentages indicate that there was a glass ceiling in the business world?

Yet, some notable and pioneering women have succeeded in rising to the top in spite of barriers and prejudices. The appearance of women in banks, for example, was the biggest revolution in the twentieth-century story of banking, and it was inevitable that some of them would be promoted to managerial roles.

- In 1973, Stella Brummel was the managing director of Benford Ltd. – the largest manufacturer of concrete-making equipment in the UK and she was voted the first 'Businesswoman of the Year'.

- In 1984, Brenda Dean became the first woman to be the head of a major trade union: as general Secretary of SOGAT (Society of Graphical and Allied Trades).

SOURCE 6

Hilda Harding, the first female bank manager, working in a London branch of Barclays in 1958

- Karren Brady was just 23 when she was appointed Managing Director of Birmingham City Football Club. Between 1993 and 2009 she turned the Club's fortunes around and in October 2009 her business was valued at over £82 million. She appears on television as Lord Alan Sugar's right-hand woman in *The Apprentice*.

- Eliza Manningham-Buller worked in espionage for 30 years before becoming the head of MI5 (2002-06). She oversaw the transformation of MI5 and doubled the number of staff employed.

Karren Brady

In Wales, due to the need for diversification in difficult times, some women farmers have managed to transform the fortunes of their farm economies and turn them into successful businesses. During a freak snowstorm in 1982, Rachel Rowlands found herself with gallons of spare milk and no prospect that tankers could reach her farm at Brynllys, near Aberystwyth, for ten days. She revived a traditional family recipe and produced organic yoghurt, which became a household name throughout Britain, 'Rachel's Organic Dairy'. Likewise, in 1987, Thelma Adams and her husband, Gwynfor, faced with a glut of milk because of the European Commission's milk quotas, began to produce Caerffili and Cenarth cheese at their farm near Boncath, in Carmarthenshire.

The venture was a huge success and the cheeses were soon for sale at Harrods in London.

In the meantime, several initiatives have been launched to encourage women to participate fully in business. In 1992 Opportunity 2000 was established to sign up companies committed to improving the quality and quantity of women's participation in the workforce. In Wales there have been several other initiatives including *Chwarae Teg* (1992) and *MEWN Cymru* (Minority Ethnic Women's Network), both of which emphasise training and the importance of childcare to facilitate women to achieve their potential in the workplace.

TASK

Identify and research the career of a successful businesswoman, since the 1960s.

Opportunities in radio and television

Some pioneering women had been involved in radio from its early years. Hilda Matheson was the BBC's first Director of Talks in 1926 and Ethel Snowden was appointed to its Board of Governors in the same year. Both women clashed with the Director General, John Reith. In 1935 Sheila Borrett became the first female national radio announcer, but she only lasted three months because of the countless complaints, mainly from women listeners, that she lacked authority!

Although women were tolerated as announcers and presenters on the radio for the duration of the war, the post-war period did not bring many rewards. However, Mary Malcolm did succeed in transferring from radio to BBC television, where she worked as an announcer from 1948 to 1954. Others, such as Barbara Mandell – ITV, 1955 and Nan Winton – BBC 1960, were even allowed to be occasional newsreaders, a post considered to be among the most prestigious by broadcasters. Another very important pioneer was Joan Bakewell, who presented *Late Night Line-up* on BBC 2 from 1965 to 1975. In the meantime, Sheila Tracy had become the first successful female newsreader on Radio 4. All these women showed the way for others who wished to break through the 'glass ceiling' in broadcasting. However, many of these successful female employees were unmarried or married and childless.

Mary Malcolm, the post-war television announcer and one of the first women to grace the country's living rooms

The report listed some of the objections of male staff in the BBC to women as newsreaders and news reporters:

- a woman's voice attracts too much attention. ... [there is] the problem of women having unsuitable 'Lah-di-dah' voices ...

- [The feelings of the Editor of Radio News ... was that ... women are simply not able to do hard news stories as they] see themselves as experts on women's features.

Angela Holdsworth, one of the first female TV documentary producers in the 1970s, in an interview with historian Suzanne Franks in 2006, reported that the Heads of News and Current Affairs in 1974, all male, had said firmly: 'how could a woman possibly break news of wars, genocide, rail disasters? She wouldn't be taken seriously; people would be looking at her ear-rings or hair-do.'

Meryl O'Keefe, a presenter on World Service News from 1975, in an interview with Suzanne Franks in 2006, said that previously women had been considered 'too emotional' for such a post.

From documents at the BBC Written Archive Centre and from Suzanne Franks' paper 'Attitudes to Women in the BBC in the 1970s – not so much a glass ceiling as one of reinforced concrete', 2011

By the early 1970s, however, the BBC was aware that it was not reflecting the true spirit of the age in this respect. Therefore, in 1973, it commissioned a confidential internal report, *Limitations to the Recruitment and Advancement of Women in the BBC*, which highlighted the problems that faced its female employees and the often hostile attitudes towards them.

In spite of these attitudes, however, on 18 April 1975, Angela Rippon became a regular presenter of BBC One's flagship news programme *Nine O'clock News*, a role she fulfilled until 1981. She was well aware of her responsibilities: 'I knew if I made a hash of it no woman would be allowed another chance for at least five years'. Others followed, notably Anna Ford on ITN in 1978 and Moira Stewart, the first African-Carribean female national television newsreader in 1981.

However, current affairs programmes still lagged behind. The breakthrough came when Sue Lawley worked on *Tonight* and *Nationwide* and when Sue MacGregor became one of the regular hosts on the hard news Radio 4 *Today* programme in 1984. MacGregor did not realise until many years later that she was being paid £20,000 less than her male colleagues for doing the same work. The Sims Report of 1985 into 'Women in BBC Management' recommended full maternity rights, job share schemes and workplace nurseries, among other incentives to bring women into top jobs at the BBC.

Barriers crashed and taboos lay shattered when Angela Rippon became a regular presenter of BBC One's Nine O'clock News *in 1975*

It is interesting to note that women progressed more quickly into important roles in the independent media. Eirwen Davies worked as a Welsh-language newsreader and announcer for TWW and Harlech television in the late 1950s and 60s, although she was banned for a time because the programme controller at TWW felt that, as a female, she "lacked authority".

Since this challenging period, women have succeeded in many important posts in broadcasting. In Wales, for example, Menna Richards was appointed Director of BBC Cymru Wales (2000-2010), earning a salary of £185,000 a year in 2009.

One issue that caused a furore in 2010-11 was the treatment of older, more mature female presenters. Former Countryfile presenter, 53 year old Miriam O'Reilly, won a case of age discrimination against the BBC. Several other successful journalists, presenters and newsreaders joined in the campaign and supported her cause including Miriam O'Reilly, Gloria Hunniford, Baroness (Joan) Bakewell, Angela Rippon, Jo Whiley, Jennie Bond and Arlene Phillips

Menna Richards, Director of BBC Cymru Wales 2000-2010

TASKS

1. Discuss the main objections that were raised against female broadcasters.
2. Outline the main steps taken in challenging the 'glass ceiling' by female broadcasters in this period.

Yet, in many other aspects of media coverage, women did, and do, not get a fair share of the cake. Although individual women athletes, gymnasts and tennis players are featured quite abundantly during major tournaments and games, popular female team sports, such as netball, hockey, football or rugby, are hardly ever seen on television. Contrast this with the number of hours devoted to male team games in a week's television viewing. In 2011 the BBC Sports Personality of the Year award was soundly criticised for not including any women on its 10-person shortlist.

A cartoon by Jacky Fleming illustrating the frustrations of many talented female team players

Women on the BBC Sports Personality of the Year shortlists:

- 2011: No-one
- 2010: Jessica Ennis (third), Amy Williams
- 2009: Jessica Ennis (third), Beth Tweddle
- 2008: Rebecca Adlington (third), Nicole Cooke, Christine Ohuruogu, Rebecca Romero
- 2007: Paula Radcliffe, Christine Ohuruogu
- 2006: Zara Phillips (winner), Beth Tweddle (third), Nicole Cooke

TASK

Consider why sportswomen find it difficult to be accepted in broadcasting.

Women fashion designers

During the last fifty years Britain has produced women fashion designers who have certainly broken through the glass ceiling. The fashion designer, Mary Quant, who is of Welsh parentage, has been credited with popularising the miniskirt in the 1960s. The 'mini' revolutionised women's lives by bringing fun and fantasy into fashion and by encouraging young women to dress to please themselves. She typified the mood of the Swinging Sixties with her knee-high white plastic boots, her heavy eyeliner make-up and her plastic raincoats.

Zandra Rhodes was another innovator, with her dramatic but feminine designs and theatrical use of colour. Rhodes was chosen as Designer of the Year in 1972. Vivienne Westwood also lived and worked in London in the 1970s and contributed greatly to the vibrant fashion scene. Westwood was greatly influenced by the punk style and she incorporated safety pins and bicycle chains into her designs. All three women were truly pioneering creative designers and, at the same time, immensely successful businesswomen.

SOURCE 14

Mary Quant, the iconic fashion designer in the 1960s

TASK

Research the careers of other female fashion designer or top models and discuss whether they have succeeded in smashing the glass ceiling in their professions.

Women in education

As we have seen, teaching has been one of the most important professions for women, and Welsh women in particular, throughout the twentieth century. Yet few of these very successful teachers went on to become head teachers. In the secondary sector, with the introduction of comprehensive schools and the closure of girls' grammar schools from the 1960s onwards, Wales lost a whole generation of able and formidable female head teachers.

However some headway has been made in increasing the number of female head teachers in both sectors during the last decades. One outstanding achievement occurred in the mid-1970s when Betty Campbell became the first black female primary head in Wales – at Mount Stuart Primary School in Cardiff. In 1990, 41% of the primary school heads in Wales were female; in 1996/7 the percentage had risen to 47%. In the secondary sector the equivalent percentages were much lower at 8.3% and 11.8% respectively, but had reached 19% by 2007. During the first decade of the twenty-first century, however, women have made inroads into the School Inspectorate system in Wales: Susan Lewis was Chief Inspector of Education and Training between 1997 and 2009 and was succeeded by Ann Keane, a Welsh-speaker from Carmarthenshire.

Betty [Campbell] has faced prejudice throughout her life and has overcome many obstacles ... be it education departments or politicians. As a result of setting herself goals and taking positive action to achieve them, she eventually succeeded in her campaign to become headmistress of Mount Stuart School in Cardiff Bay. ...
She demonstrates that with determination, honesty and passion you can achieve your goals.

Introduction to Betty Campbell, the first black primary head teacher in Wales, at a conference in Cardiff, 2011

In higher education the scene is evolving from year to year. In Wales and England in 1985, 42% of the undergraduates were female, but only 15% of the lecturers and 3% of the professors were women. In Wales the percentages were persistently lower. Several pioneering women did manage to crack the glass ceiling, however, and become professors, even in the early years of the University of Wales, and during the second half of the twentieth century many more have joined their ranks as leaders of Welsh universities. Among them are:

- Deirdre Beddoe, who was appointed the first female professor of Women's Studies at the Polytechnic of Wales (later Glamorgan University) in 1989;

- Professor Teresa Rees, the first female Pro Vice-Chancellor of Cardiff University in 2004;

- Julie Lydon took up the position of Vice-Chancellor of Glamorgan University in 2010;

- Professor April McMahon commenced as Vice-Chancellor of Aberystwyth University in 2011.

Professor April McMahon, appointed Vice-Chancellor of Aberystwyth University in 2011, a native of the Scottish Borders, who has made considerable progress in learning spoken Welsh in under a year in her new post

Although these appointments show that women with great ability and determination can crack the glass ceiling in the university sector, a great deal still remains to be done to ensure that women are equally represented in top jobs in education. Even in 2008, although women make up 42.3% of the academic university staff, only 17.5% of them are professors.

It was not until the recommendations of the Goodenough report, implemented through the National Health Act in 1948, that all medical schools were obliged to admit women; and they did so for many years subject to stringent quotas, usually around 15%-20%. However, the numbers of women admitted to medical schools have risen slowly and by the early 1980s 50% of the intake were women. As a result, in 2007, 28% of all consultants and 42% of all General Practitioners were female.

It seems that towards the end of the first decade of the twenty-first century the situation is really changing. Having successful female role models has been a crucial and positive influence.

TASK

Outline the main achievements of women in education and the challenges that still face them in trying to break through 'the glass ceiling'.

THE SUCCESS OF FEMALE ROLE MODELS

Laura Ashley (1925-1985)

Laura Ashley became a household name as a fashion designer and manufacturer of a range of colourful and feminine fabrics for clothes and home furnishing.

Laura Ashley, the iconic fashion designer at work in the 1980s

Born in Dowlais, Merthyr Tydfil in 1925 she later moved to London. She left school at 16 and served in the Women's Royal Navy Service (WRNS) during the war. She married Bernard Ashley in 1949 and became the mother of four children. As a young, housebound mother in the 1950s, she began to design head scarves and napkins etc. on the kitchen table of her attic flat in Pimlico, and her husband took charge of the printing. She drew the inspiration for her printed fabrics from a display of traditional crafts at the Victoria and Albert Museum in London.

In 1955, the Laura Ashley Company was formed and factories were opened in Carno, and later in Newtown, Powys, to produce the goods. The family moved to Machynlleth in the early 1960s and from there to Carno. She designed her first dress in 1966 and this increased the popularity of the company hugely. The first Laura Ashley shop was opened in South Kensington two years later. Soon, her designs were selling around the world and by 1979 the company's turnover was £25

million. Her success depended very much upon the partnership with her husband, Bernard. She had the magical ability and flair to design fabrics and clothes that were immensely popular with her customers and Bernard had the expertise in business.

When Laura Ashley died in an accident in 1985, the company had some 5,000 outlets worldwide stocking her products. The family home at Rhydoldog, near Rhaeadr, which was furnished in the trademark floral designs that gained worldwide popularity in the mid 1980s, became the base for the Laura Ashley Foundation, the organization established in memory of the designer and which distributes funding to worthy causes, particularly in rural mid-Wales.

Laura Ashley's life proves that a woman can create a successful global business from humble beginnings.

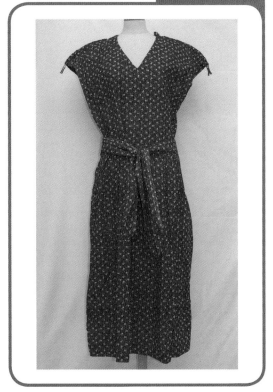

A typical Laura Ashley dress in printed fabric, c.1980

J. K. Rowling (born 1965)

The author, J.K.Rowling (Joanne Rowling) was born in 1965 in Yate, Gloucestershire and spent much of her childhood near Chepstow, Monmouthshire. She studied French and Classics at Exeter University and then taught English in Portugal, where she got married and had her first child. Soon afterwards she was divorced. On returning to Britain, she enrolled on a teacher training course at Edinburgh University and found life very difficult and challenging as a single mother.

SOURCE 19

Author, J.K. Rowling

Rowling conceived of the idea for her first novel in the Harry Potter series on a train journey between Manchester and London in 1990. Eventually, after several rejections, her first book, *Harry Potter and the Philosopher's Stone*, was accepted for publication by Bloomsbury Press and appeared in 1997. Six others followed in quick succession. The last, *Harry Potter and the Deathly Hallows*, was the fastest-selling book of all time, selling 11 million copies on the first day of its release in the UK and USA. Her books have been acclaimed for their imagination, humour, simple, direct style and clever plot constructions. They have sold around 450 million copies worldwide and have been translated into 67 languages, which includes the Welsh translation of the first book. They have also been adapted into immensely successful films and video games. Rowling insisted that the films had to be filmed in Britain, with British actors.

SOURCE 20

(i) It is our choices, Harry, that show what we truly are, far more than our abilities.

(ii) it matters not what someone is born, but what they grow to be.

Two quotes by J.K.Rowling, which explain her philosophy and illustrate why she is seen as a good role model for young people:
(i) Harry Potter and the Chamber of Secrets
(ii) Harry Potter and the Goblet of Fire

In 2007, *Time* magazine named her as runner-up for its 'Person of the Year' award, noting the social, moral and political inspiration she had given to others. A year later the *Sunday Times Rich List* estimated her fortune at £560 million. She remarried in 2001 to Dr Neil Murray and they have two children.

Rowling supports many charities that reflect her own life and interests. In 2000, she established the Volant Charitable Trust, which funds research into Multiple Sclerosis (of which her mother died), and charities and projects, whether national or community-based, at home or abroad, that alleviate social deprivation, with a particular emphasis on women's and children's issues. Again this is a reminder of the difficult period she endured as a lone parent at the turn of the millennium.

J.K.Rowling is an excellent female role model because she conquered personal adversities and has used her 'rags to riches' life story to inspire others. She has used her new-found wealth to help others in a positive and **philanthropic** way.

Anita Roddick (1942-2007)

SOURCE 21

Anita Roddick, founder of The Body Shop

Anita Roddick was born of Italian parents in Littlehampton, Sussex in 1942. She failed her 11+ and attended a secondary modern school, but eventually trained as a teacher, before setting out to work on a **kibbutz** in Israel for a year and then on a trip around the world. These experiences led her to question the normal practices found in retailing, especially the importance of recycling, protecting the environment and producing goods in the most ethical way possible. In the 1970s these were not very popular or acceptable ideas in the business world.

Her first venture, The Body Shop, began in 1976 in a very modest way. She produced a range of 15 hand-made cosmetics in her kitchen and sold them in recyclable urine sample bottles in a shop in Brighton. Her husband, Gordon, meantime, had gone on a trekking adventure through North and South America and left her to fend for herself and her two daughters.

His only advice had been to try to take at least £300 worth of sales a week. When he returned, however, he proved to be the financial brain required to run the new business and Anita could concentrate upon expanding the range of products and being the passionate public face of the company and an environmental campaigner. During the following years she campaigned on behalf of animal welfare, the protection of the Brazilian rainforests and against Third World poverty. To do so she worked with and supported charities such as Greenpeace, Amnesty International and was a co-founder of the *Big Issue*, the newspaper sold by and for homeless people.

The Body Shop took as its mission: 'To dedicate our business to the pursuit of social and environmental change'. The shops became icons of the 1980s High Streets. In 1999 the company, established in 1984, was valued at £800 million. By 2004 it had over 2000 shops, serving 77 million customers in 51 countries. However, in 2006 the company was purchased by the L'Oréal Group for £652 million, a move that was heavily criticised because this company had a very low rating for animal testing of its cosmetics.

A year later Anita Roddick died. She had been given a contaminated blood transfusion in 1971 and this had led to her contracting Hepatitis C, which contributed to her untimely death. She left £51 million of her fortune to charity.

This remarkable campaigner and entrepreneur is a successful female role model who has set an example for other aspiring women to follow.

TASKS

1. Why do you think these three role models have been so successful? Are there any common themes that you can identify?
2. Identify and research other successful female role models during this period.

Examination practice

This section provides guidance on how to answer question 2(a) from Units 1 and 2. The question is worth 5 marks.

Question 2(a) – the understanding of a key feature through the selection of appropriate knowledge

Describe how successful women role models have been important for female employment.

[5 marks]

Tips on how to answer

- Make sure you only include information that is **directly relevant.**
- Jot down your initial thoughts, making a list of the points you intend to mention.
- After you have finished your list try to put the points into **chronological order** by numbering them.
- It is a good idea to start your answer using the words from the question. E.g. 'Women role models have been important for female employment…'
- Try to include **specific factual details** such as dates, events, and the names of key people. The more informed your description the higher the mark you will receive.

Response by candidate one

Successful female role models have done a lot for female employment. They have shown what can be done with hard work and a positive attitude and this has encouraged other women to follow their example.

Examiner's comment

This is a very generalised answer. It attempts to answer the question but lacks specific knowledge about the topic such as key figures. It only makes one worthwhile observation and would be given 1 mark.

Response by candidate two

Successful women role models have encouraged other women to follow their example. Laura Ashley was a very successful businesswoman who established a very successful range of women's wear and later expanded her business to cover home and furniture. She had a factory in Carno in Mid Wales and opened her first shop in Llanidloes. She showed other women that it was possible to change a small cottage industry into an international company with 5000 outlets worldwide. She showed other women that it was possible to create a strong commercial brand. She proved that women could be hard headed and that women could be successful in business if they were properly motivated and that they could compete in a man's world. In many ways she is a heroine for other women within the world of work. Anita Roddick may well have been inspired by Laura Ashley's business sense.

Examiner's comment

This is a developed answer. There is clear focus upon answering the question with a good range of specific factual detail. There is a sense of chronology within the answer and clear links to the question. This is a level 2 response worthy of 4 marks.

Now you have a go

Describe how changes in secondary and higher education after the Second World War benefitted women in employment.

[4 marks]

CHAPTER 7

HOW MUCH SUCCESS DID WOMEN ACHIEVE IN THE FIGHT FOR POLITICAL RIGHTS IN WALES AND ENGLAND IN THE EARLY TWENTIETH CENTURY?

Introduction

SOURCE 1

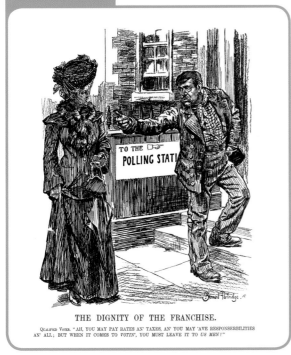

THE DIGNITY OF THE FRANCHISE.

QUALIFIED VOTER. "AH, YOU MAY PAY RATES AN' TAXES, AN' YOU MAY 'AVE RESPONSIBILITIES AN' ALL.; BUT WHEN IT COMES TO *VOTIN'*, YOU MUST LEAVE IT TO *US MEN*!"

A cartoon published in Punch *magazine, May 1905*

TASK

What does Source 1 show you about attitudes towards granting women the right to vote in the early twentieth century?

In Victorian society a woman's place was seen to be in the home. Women were expected to concentrate upon areas at which they were considered to be good, namely domestic service, raising children and looking after the household. Men dealt with political issues and in 1900 women were not allowed to vote. This situation did not change until 1918 when, after a sustained campaign by female activists, women over 30 were granted the right to vote.

SUFFRAGISTS AND SUFFRAGETTES

Origins of the campaign to obtain voting rights for women

During the 1860s the **women's suffrage** movement began to emerge with the establishment of suffrage organizations in five major cities – London, Manchester, Bristol, Birmingham and Edinburgh. They adopted peaceful campaigns: collecting petitions, lobbying MPs and holding meetings. When the1867 Reform Act was being debated in parliament the Liberal Reformer, John Stuart Mill, put forward the argument that women householders should be allowed to vote in general elections alongside men. While his radical views met with little support among fellow MPs, the late nineteenth century did see increasing debate about whether women should be allowed the vote.

SOURCE 2

to lay a ground for refusing the suffrage to any one, it is necessary to allege either personal unfitness or public danger. ... Can it be pretended that women who manage an estate or conduct a business – who pay rates and taxes ... are not capable of a function of which every male householder is capable?

Part of a speech made by the Liberal MP, John Stuart Mill, to parliament in May 1867 during the debate for the passing of the 1867 Reform Act. Mill was a reformer (Hansard, HC Deb 20 May 1867 vol 187, cc779-852)

SOURCE 3

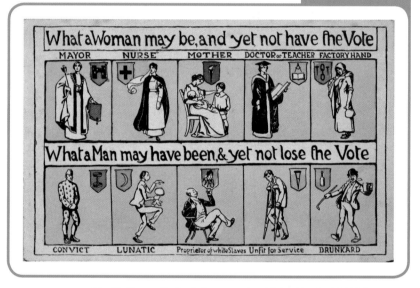

The 'Suffrage Atelier'. A postcard published by the NUWSS in the early 1900s, highlighting the injustices of the voting system

Arguments for and against granting women the right to vote:

For	Against
• Women pay taxes just like men do and so should be allowed to say how the government spends those taxes;	• The belief that women lacked the capacity to make rational political decisions – the MP John Bright argued that women were, by nature and intellect, unfit to vote, being too emotional;
• Women can own property and should have equality with men to enable them to vote;	• Politics was seen as men's business and women should concentrate upon looking after their families and home;
• Women who own property can already vote in county council and parish elections and they have proved that they can be trusted with the vote;	• Women would be corrupted by politics, it would take away their innocence and it would be improper to solicit their vote;
• The Reform Acts of 1867 and 1884 meant that 60% of adult males were now enfranchised – denying the vote to women was increasingly seen as being discriminatory;	• As women's interests were already safeguarded and represented in parliament by men, granting them the vote would be wasted as they would only vote according to their husband's or father's instructions;

For	Against
• The decisions made by parliament affect men and women so women should be allowed to vote for the MPs who pass those laws; • The belief that female influence at the ballot box and in parliament would advance the interests of women and serve to promote reforms such as improvement in educational provision, the opportunity to enter professions currently reserved to men, the improvement in property rights and working conditions.	• If the vote was given to women then it would have to be extended to everyone; • Granting the vote to women would destroy family life and undermine the existing social order, as women who engaged in politics would not marry, not have children and the human race would die out; • Women lacked the physical strength to fight for their country and therefore should not have a say in whether their country went to war.

The problem facing the women suffrage movement was that some prominent MPs like Gladstone, Joseph Chamberlain, Kipling and H. H. Asquith were all very opposed to the idea of granting the vote to women. While some Conservative and Liberal MPs did support the female cause, such as the Welsh Liberal MP, T. E. Ellis, their political parties were worried that **enfranchised** females would vote for their opponents and so took no action. There was the fear that granting the vote would just lead to demands for further reforms.

By the early twentieth century there were three main groupings of suffrage campaigners in Britain, the largest two being the NUWSS (National Union of Women's Suffrage Societies) and the WSPU (Women's Social and Political Union). Although their aims were the same, they went about campaigning for the vote in completely different ways. Members of these organizations came to be known by the more popular labels of Suffragists and Suffragettes.

SOURCE 4

I do not see why, because a small set of demonstrative women persisted in setting up what they claimed as the rights of their sex, the House should force upon the more numerous and more retiring section of the female community what they did not wish for, and would, if given to them, probably repudiate.

Part of speech given by J. H. Scourfield, the Conservative MP for Pembrokeshire, in the House of Commons, 3 May 1871 (Hansard, HC Deb 03 May 1871 vol 206, cc68-123)

TASKS

1. How far does Source 3 support the view that the voting system was unfair to women?

2. How useful is Source 4 to an historian studying the attitudes of some MPs towards granting women the right to vote?

3. Why do Sources 2 and 4 have different views about whether women should be allowed to vote?

4. Write a newspaper article summarising the arguments for and against allowing women the right to vote.

The Suffragists (the moderates)

In 1897 Millicent Fawcett formed the National Union of Women's Suffrage Societies (NUWSS), which brought together all the different societies that had been formed across the country over the previous three decades. Its members were called Suffragists and they believed in putting forward a good argument before MPs and the British public and using peaceful, moderate methods to secure the vote:

- Lobbying of MPs by writing thousands of letters, exerting particular pressure on Liberal and later Labour MPs;
- Attending meetings of all political parties and asking questions about women's suffrage;
- Organizing petitions;
- Holding public meetings;
- Organizing rallies and marches;
- Publishing their own newspaper, *The Women's Franchise*, to help spread their message.

Such actions did win some political support. J. H. Griffith ('*Y Gohebydd*' [The Correspondent]) used his position as the London correspondent for the radical Welsh newspaper *Baner ac Amserau Cymru* to support the suffragists in Welsh periodicals. The NUWSS grew into a large organization and membership increased from 6000 in 1907, to 16,000 in 1909 and over 100,000 members in over 600 societies around the country by 1914. Support was strongest in the industrialised regions of England but 28 societies were established across Wales, the first being at Llandudno in 1907. Other branches included those at Aberystwyth, Bangor (1909), Bargoed, Bridgend, Cardiff (1908), Carmarthen, Caernarvon (1910), Dolgellau, Lampeter, Llanelli, Merthyr, Pontypridd, Rhyl (1908) and Swansea.

SOURCE 5

the ... list [of NUWSS branches] shows clearly that Wales was no back-water when it came to votes for women. In fact, by the eve of the First World War, Cardiff was the largest women's suffrage society outside of London, a position which it sought to maintain in rivalry with Glasgow.

Deirdre Beddoe, 'Women and Politics in Twentieth Century Wales', which was the Annual Lecture given to the Welsh Political Archive in 2004

Millicent Garrett Fawcett (1847-1929)

- Born 1847, the seventh of ten children of an East Anglican corn and coal merchant;
- Received no formal education except for a short period at a school at Blackheath, London;
- 1867: married Henry Fawcett, a Professor of Economics at Cambridge and a Liberal MP who supported the 1867 Reform Bill and was a supporter of John Stuart Mill;
- Promoted women's education at Cambridge leading to the founding of a women's college, Newnham, in 1871;
- 1867: joined the first Women's Suffrage Committee;
- Worked to secure the legal right for married women to their own property;
- 1897: formed the NUWSS and became its first president;
- 1905-14: opposed the militant suffragettes;
- 1914-18: suspended the campaign for votes and encouraged women's war work;
- 1919: retired from presidency of the NUWSS after the granting of the vote to women over 30;
- Lived to see the extension of female franchise in 1928.

After 1907 over twenty different suffrage societies were formed, the third largest being the Women's Freedom League (WFL), which was set up in Swansea in 1909. Within Wales it had offices at Swansea, Aberdare, Barry, Cardiff and Montgomery by 1913.

Workers have been sent about the factory districts to hold open-air meetings and to speak to the women at the factory-gates and in their own houses. The work is necessarily slow as the area to be covered is very large, but all the workers report themselves convinced that the women feel a real interest in the subject, many of them, particularly those who are rate-payers, keenly resent their exclusion from the Franchise. ... There is no difficulty in obtaining signatures – only a very small proportion refuse to sign, – but there is a great deal of hard work involved going from house to house in the evening, after factory hours, holding cottage meetings and collecting signatures. One encouraging fact in the work has been the number of men who have shown themselves in sympathy with the women's claims.

An account of how suffragists attempted to recruit members in the textile towns of the north of England. It appears in The National Union of Women's Suffrage Societies' report of the Executive Committee of the North of England's Society for Women's Suffrage (Annual Report 1899-1900, presented at the annual meeting on 28 November 1900)

I was already deeply interested in the work of the National Union of Women Suffrage Societies ... so I decided to take a job ... and became Secretary to the National Union of Women's Suffrage Societies. ... I dealt with the correspondence, produced the Union's paper, of which I became the editor, and learned by experience how to select, produce and edit material ...

I had an exciting year of office organising petitions, deputations, processions

The memories of suffragist Dame Margery Corbett Ashby. She joined the NUWSS while still a student at Cambridge University

However, this passive, law-abiding campaign was criticised by some women as being too slow and ineffective. The result was the formation of a breakaway movement – the WSPU.

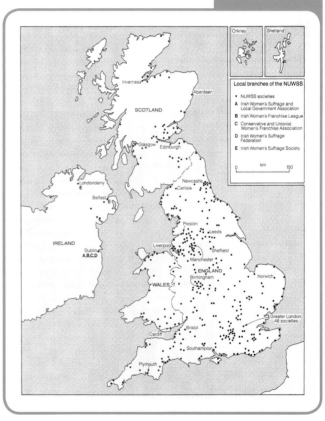

A map showing the NUWSS societies in 1914

1. What does Source 8 show you about support for the NUWSS in 1914?

2. Use Source 5 and your own knowledge to explain the support for the NUWSS in Wales.

3. Describe the methods used by the NUWSS in their campaign to obtain the vote. You may wish to use Sources 6 and 7 for information.

4. How important was Millicent Fawcett in the campaign by women to obtain political rights?

The Suffragettes (the militants)

In 1903 Emmeline Pankhurst broke from the law-abiding suffragists to form the Women's Social and Political Union (WSPU). The WSPU believed in direct action and it adopted a violent, militant style of campaigning. In 1906 the *Daily Mail* newspaper called its members *the suffragettes*, a name that stuck. The WSPU became the second largest suffrage organization and its leading members were:

- Emmeline Pankhurst and her daughters Christabel and Sylvia;
- Annie Kenney;
- Emmeline Pethick Lawrence;
- Hannah Mitchell.

we determined to organise a society of women to demand immediate enfranchisement ... through political action. ...
    We resolved to limit our membership exclusively to women ... and to be satisfied with nothing but action on our question. Deeds, not words, was to be our permanent motto.

Mrs Emmeline Pankhurst, My Own Story *(1914)*

The election of a Liberal government in 1906 gave encouragement to the WSPU who hoped that the new MPs would be more sympathetic to their cause than the previous Conservative governments. They were soon to be disappointed by the anti-reform attitudes of the Prime Minister Campbell-Bannerman (1906-08) and his successor H. H. Asquith (1908-16). As a result, the WSPU began to adopt more violent and militant tactics to draw attention to their cause. The WSPU was not as widely represented in Wales as the NUWSS and by 1913 it had only five branches in the country – Newport, Pontypool, Griffithstown, Cardiff and Barry.

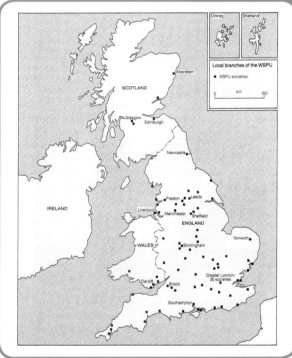

A map showing WSPU branches in 1914

Emmeline Pankhurst (1859-1928)

- Born 1858 in Manchester into a radical political family;
- 1879: married Dr. Richard Pankhurst, a radical Manchester lawyer who supported the rights of women;
- An active member of various suffragist organizations;
- 1903: founded the WSPU;
- Her three daughters all became members of the WSPU;
- 1905: began to use more militant forms of protest;
- 1908: imprisoned in Holloway jail;
- 1912-14: constantly arrested, released as a result of hunger-striking and re-arrested;
- 1914-18 maintained a truce to militancy during the First World War;
- 1918: took little part in the agitation leading to the first instalment of women's suffrage.

The women of the WSPU used very different tactics from those followed by the NUWSS. They aimed for maximum publicity and were prepared to break the law and go to prison for their cause. They heckled politicians, attacked property, smashed windows, damaged paintings, chained themselves to railings and burned down buildings. From 1907, to help spread their message, they printed their own weekly newspaper called *Votes for Women*.

SOURCE 11

Wales ... was to play centre stage in the militant years of 1912 and 1913 because it was the home of prominent members of the government and attracted suffragettes from outside. In June 1912 a London suffragette leapt out before the home secretary and North Monmouthshire MP Reginald McKenna, who was accompanying the king and queen on a visit to Llandaff cathedral. But it was Lloyd George, chancellor of the exchequer, who drew English suffragettes like a magnet. They challenged the great man in the Liberal heartland, confronting him at Caernarfon, Wrexham and Llanystumdwy in 1912.

Deirdre Beddoe, 'Women and Politics in Twentieth Century Wales', which was the Annual Lecture given to the Welsh Political Archive in 2004

TASKS

1. Explain why the WSPU was formed in 1903.

2. Use Source 11 and your own knowledge to explain why Wales played an important part in the militancy campaign of 1912-13.

3. How important was Emmeline Pankhurst in the campaign to secure the vote for women?

'Deeds, not words'

Between 1905 and 1913 the WSPU campaigned using increasingly violent methods. To begin with they engaged in minor public disorder offences, which involved heckling, questioning and embarrassing Liberal MPs and government ministers.

In October 1905 Christabel Pankhurst and Annie Kenney were arrested after a Liberal meeting in Manchester's Free Trade Hall when they interrupted a speech given by Sir Edward Grey by shouting 'Will the Liberal Government give the vote to women?' In October of the following year ten suffragettes were arrested and later imprisoned for refusing to pay fines following a protest at the opening of parliament.

In June 1908 the WSPU staged a 'Women's Sunday' in Hyde Park, which drew a crowd of 500,000 people. That same month 122 suffragettes were arrested after disturbances in Parliament Square. Twenty-nine women were sent to prison, including the first two 'window-smashers', Mary Leigh and Edith New. Edith New had also chained herself to the railings of No. 10 Downing Street.

SOURCE 12

- MPs heckled
- Protest meetings and marches
- Slogans painted on walls
- Women chained to railings
- Windows smashed
- Reservoirs polluted with dye
- Golf courses damaged with acid
- Hunger-strikes
- Arson attacks
- Chemicals poured into post boxes
- Cutting telegraph wires

Methods of militant protest

SOURCE 13

last night a carefully organised band of Suffragists carried out ... a window-breaking campaign in the principal streets of the West-end ...

For a quarter of an hour or twenty minutes nothing was heard ... but the fall of shattered glass ...

The attack was begun practically simultaneously ... It was one of the busiest periods of the day – the half-hour before the shops closed for the night. Suddenly, women and girls who had a moment before appeared to be on peaceful shopping expeditions produced from bags or from muffs hammers, stones, and sticks, and began an attack upon the nearest windows

A report on organised window smashing, which appeared in The Daily Telegraph on Saturday 2 March 1912

When the National Eisteddfod of Wales was held at the Royal Albert Hall in London in June 1909, the presidential address delivered by the Prime Minister, Asquith, during the crowning ceremony of the bard was interrupted by a suffragette. At the same event Mrs Pethwick-Lawrence chained her leg to one of the seats. Likewise, the National Eisteddfod held in Wrexham in 1912 was interrupted by militant protests.

During 1909 imprisoned militants in Holloway prison started a campaign of hunger strikes and the authorities responded by force-feeding them. A large demonstration held in London on 18 November 1910 turned into a riot when the police and men from the crowd of onlookers assaulted the protestors. The incident became known as 'Black Friday'.

Despite such incidents militant action continued. On 17 June 1911 a crowd of 60,000 suffragettes staged the 'Women's Coronation Procession' to coincide with the coronation of King George V. During 1912 and 1913 the protests became more extreme. Lloyd-George's new house in Surrey was damaged after a fire-bomb attack in February 1913. Telephone and telegraph wires were cut at Queen Street Station in Cardiff and at Llantarnam. Wales's most radical suffragette was Margaret Haig Mackworth:

SOURCE 14

Margaret Haig Mackworth, later Lady Rhondda ... who set up the Newport branch of the WSPU, broke every taboo of her class – selling the organization's newspaper, *Votes for Women*, on Newport High Street; speaking on public platforms including that of Merthyr Liberal Club, where she was pelted with herrings and tomatoes; jumping on the running-board of Prime Minister Asquith's car and blowing up a pillar box on Risca Road, Newport in 1913. For this last act she was imprisoned and went on hunger-strike.

Deirdre Beddoe, 'Women and Politics in Twentieth Century Wales', which was the Annual Lecture given to the Welsh Political Archive in 2004

On 8 June 1913 Emily Wilding Davison became the only suffragette martyr. During the Derby at Epsom racecourse she dashed out onto the racetrack and was trampled to the ground by the King's horse, Anmer. She died four days later in hospital from head wounds.

SOURCE 15

Emily Wilding Davison was struck by the King's horse, Anmer, at the Epsom Derby on 4 June 1913

SOURCE 16

The result of an arson attack by suffragettes on Lady White's house on 20 March 1913. Lady White was a well-known opponent of women's suffrage

TASKS

1. What does Source 16 tell you about the activities of the suffragettes?
2. Describe the methods of militant protest used by the suffragettes.
3. How useful is Source 13 to the historian studying the actions of the suffragettes?
4. How far does Source 15 support the view that the suffragettes believed in 'Deeds, not words'?

How did the Government respond to the pressure for female enfranchisement?

When Herbert Asquith became the new Liberal Prime Minister in April 1908, he appeared to be totally opposed to the idea of votes for women. He was not convinced that most women wanted the vote. In June 1909 he refused a request by suffragette leaders for a meeting, and this led to an increase in militant activity.

However, a general election in 1910 did result in a less hard line policy by Asquith and following continued pressure from both the NUWSS and WSPU the Liberal Government agreed to the creation of a **Conciliation Committee**. It was made up of MPs from all parties and was to draft a Conciliation Bill to give women the vote. As a result, the WSPU called a truce to its militant actions while the Bill was being drafted and debated.

The Bill passed its first two readings with majority votes, but by May 1911 it was clear that there was insufficient parliamentary time for the Conciliation Bill to make any further progress before the summer recess. When parliament resumed in November the future of the bill looked uncertain and instead a new Reform Bill was announced, which would give the vote to men and consider the vote for women as an amendment. The WSPU reacted angrily, calling off their truce and returning to militant activity. The government was forced to withdraw its proposed Reform Bill in 1913.

However, this increased violence worked against the suffragettes. Hostility towards Lloyd-George at the opening of the Llanystumdwy Village Institute in September 1912 led to considerable violence being inflicted upon the protestors.

SOURCE 17

Lloyd George started to speak. But before he could finish one sentence a suffragette shouted, "Don't forget votes for women!" The ... crowd were angered. The people around her attacked the woman who shouted, and she finally escaped, bruised and hatless, through the edge of the crowd ...

... Lloyd George ... appealed in Welsh and English for courtesy.

Then there was another shout. ... Men around the woman struck her with fists and sticks ... Some in the crowd were shouting: "Take her to the river, boys!". ... there was no peace until the police succeeded in getting the suffragette to a nearby house.

Other suffragettes were taken by men to the village pump to cool their ardour. ... One was thrown over a bramble hedge and she and her clothes were found shred to rags.

For their own safety, some were placed under lock and key in the Church Hall, and I remember ... seeing a woman's shoe coming out of one of the windows, such was the discontent of at least one of them with the shelter that she was given.

An extract from 'Diwrnod i'w Gofio' [A Day to Remember] by O. E. Roberts, Llafar, (Summer, 1953)

SOURCE 18

Throughout this period the government continued with its policy of force-feeding suffragette prisoners on hunger strike. In April 1913 it passed the Prisoner's Temporary Discharge for Ill Health Act. This soon became known as the 'Cat and Mouse Act', as it allowed women (mice) on hunger strike to be released, recover a little and then be re-arrested by the authorities (cats) to finish their sentence.

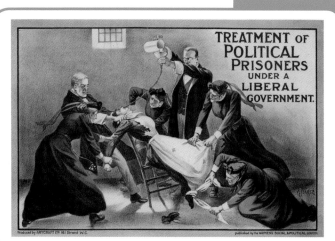

A suffragette poster from 1909 protesting about force-feeding

Handwritten on the back of this petition are the words:
Petition I took in my hand to Houses of Parliament when I got taken up   Sybil M Rhondda

Why had the vote not been gained by 1914?

By 1914, despite a high profile campaign, women had failed to secure the vote. Numerous reasons have been put forward for this:

• The Liberal Government faced a number of issues regarded as more important than votes for women: such as demand for Irish Home Rule; disestablishment of the Anglican Church in Wales; 1909 People's Budget; Parliament Bill;

• The Prime Minister, H. H. Asquith, disapproved of the actions of the suffragettes and was a major obstacle to reform;

• Their militant actions served as proof to some that the suffragettes were unfit for political responsibility;

• Growing violence of the suffragettes after 1911 antagonised and alienated more people and led to an anti-suffrage movement – the National League for Opposing Women's Suffrage, with branches in Bangor and Anglesey;

• The leadership style of Mrs Pankhurst and Christabel caused divisions within the WSPU – a breakaway movement, the WFL (Women's Freedom League) was formed in 1907 and had 4,000 members by 1914; over 100 of its members were imprisoned;

• In 1914 Sylvia Pankhurst was thrown out of the WSPU and continued her work with the East London Federation of Suffragettes.

TASKS

1. What was the aim of the Conciliation Committee?

2. Use Source 17 and your own knowledge to explain why the actions of some suffragettes caused some to dislike the movement.

3. Explain why the government introduced the 'Cat and Mouse Act' in 1913.

4. Why did the votes for women campaign fail to achieve its aims before 1914?

VOTES FOR WOMEN

The response of suffrage groups to the outbreak of war in 1914

At the outbreak of the First World War in August 1914, both the suffragists and the suffragettes suspended their campaigns in favour of the national good. Patriotism and serving their country now became a more pressing concern. The war soon produced a situation on the Home Front that provided women with new opportunities, allowing them to fill roles in society and in the work place that had previously been unattainable to them. They became van drivers, ticket collectors, tram conductors, farm labourers and munitions workers.

At first the government was slow to give women the opportunity to serve the war effort and in July 1915 the WSPU organized a rally in central London to demand the 'right to serve'. Over 30,000 women attended. Following the introduction of conscription in 1916 thousands of women were recruited to fill the jobs left vacant by men departing for the battlefields. Their willingness to take on new roles helped to change attitudes.

SOURCE 20

The women's 'Right to Serve' march in London in July 1915. David Lloyd George, Minister of Munitions, gave Emmeline Pankhurst £2,000 to stage this rally

The Speaker's Conference

With men fighting overseas for long periods, many politicians realised that the existing voting system, which required men to occupy a property for at least a year prior to an election, would now disqualify many of them from voting. How could they be expected to fight for their country yet be denied a vote? The situation needed to be addressed.

On 12 October 1916 a committee of MPs called the 'Speakers Conference' began to discuss changes to the voting system. The committee made several recommendations, one of which was to give some women the vote. A bill was drafted and was debated in the House of Commons during June 1917. It was passed by 385 votes in favour to just 55 against and the bill became law in February 1918. By this time even Asquith, the former Prime Minister, had changed his view.

SOURCE 21

Women of every station ... have proved themselves able to undertake work which before the War was regarded as solely the province of men ...Where is the man now who would deny to women the civil rights which she has earned by hard work?

Comments made by E. S. Montagu, Minister of Munitions, on 15 August 1916 (Hansard, HC Deb 15 August 1916 vol 85, cc1679-770)

SOURCE 22

I think that some years ago I ventured to use the expression, "Let the women work out their own salvation." Well, Sir, they have worked it out during this War. ... But what I confess moves me still more in this matter is the problem of reconstruction when the War is over. ... I, for my part, feel it impossible ... to withhold from women the power and the right of making their voice directly heard.

Former Prime Minister Asquith speaking on 28 March 1917. Before the war he had been opposed to votes for women (Hansard, HC Deb 28 March 1917 vol 92, cc462-524)

The Representation of the People Act, 1918

The Representation of the People Act gave the vote to all males over the age of 21 and to women over 30 who were householders or the wives of householders. It meant that 8.4 million women now gained the right to vote and they made up 39.6% of the electorate. After fifty years of campaigning women had now gained what they had been fighting for – the right to vote. Millicent Fawcett viewed this breakthrough as the greatest moment of her life. For some, however, the fact that women had to be 30 to vote yet men could vote at just 21 was an injustice, and the fight for equal suffrage rights would continue.

Christabel Pankhurst voting for the first time during the General Election of December 1918

Why did politicians appear to change their mind about giving women the vote?

The period 1914-17 witnessed a distinct change in the political climate:

- In 1915 the Liberal Government was replaced by a coalition, which contained MPs who were sympathetic to the idea of women receiving the vote;
- In December 1916 David Lloyd George, a sympathiser to the women's campaign, replaced Asquith as Prime Minister;
- The ending of the militancy campaign during the war helped to change public attitudes;

- The contribution of women to the war effort led to a call by some MPs that they should be rewarded for their efforts with the vote;
- The world was changing by 1917 and many countries had already granted women the vote: New Zealand (1893), Finland (1907), Australia (1908) and Norway (1908).

The extent to which the war was the determining factor that caused MPs to change their opinion is a matter of considerable debate among historians. Some see the war as the main driving force while others believe its importance has been over-emphasised.

The manner in which the situation was exploited owed much to the experience the women's leaders had derived from the pre-war suffrage movements; it is also true that before the war the doors to a number of professions were already slowly opening. Yet it is difficult to see how women could have achieved so much in anything like a similar time-span without the unique circumstances arising from the war.

From Arthur Marwick, an historian, writing in The Deluge: British Society and the First World War *(1991)*

Whether the war influenced the debate about votes for women is rather doubtful. ... The role played by young women in munitions factories and other formerly male employment generated excellent copy for the newspapers. But it did not lead men generally to change their ideas about gender roles. The press, the government, the unions, and the employers largely agreed in regarding women's war work as temporary. On the contrary, the war made them see women's traditional roles as wives and mothers as even more important

From Martin Pugh, an historian, writing in The March of the Women *(2000)*

TASKS

1. What does Source 23 show you about changes in the voting system in 1918?

2. How did the outbreak of war change the work of the NAWSS and WSPU?

3. Describe the Speaker's Conference of 1916-17 and its outcome.

4. Why do Sources 24 and 25 have different views about whether the First World War was the cause of MPs deciding to give women the vote in 1918?

Representation of the People (Equal Franchise) Act, 1928

After their success in 1918 many of the leading campaigners such as Emmeline Pankhurst became less involved. Christabel Pankhurst and Annie Kenney became extremely religious and Sylvia Pankhurst became involved in left-wing causes. In 1919 the NUWSS changed its name to the National Union of Societies for Equal Citizenship (NUSEC) and under its new leader, Eleanor Rathbone, it now campaigned for equal voting rights alongside other causes such as equal pay, fairer divorce laws and the opening up of the professions to women.

Despite promises to remove the inequalities in the voting ages between men and women, the governments of the 1920s were slow to act. It was left to the Conservative government of Stanley Baldwin to introduce a bill in March 1928 proposing to lower the voting age for women to 21. After passing its final vote in the Commons by 387 in favour to just 10 against, the bill became law in July 1928. After nearly seventy years of campaigning, the Representation of the People (Equal Franchise) Act finally granted equal voting rights to women.

SOURCE 26

At the Cabinet, Stanley [Baldwin] opened with a short resume [summary] of the position with regard to our pledges on the women's vote concluding that the only thing we could do was to give it all round at 21. Winston [Churchill] led the opposition with great vehemence and our opinions were then taken all the way round. I took the view with many others that 25 for both sexes would be preferable but did not think we should see it through [the Commons] and therefore favoured 21.

An extract from the diary of Leo Amery, MP for Birmingham Sparkbrook, written on 12 April 1927 (The papers of Leopold Amery, AMEL 7/21)

Women MPs in the inter-war years

Seventeen women stood as candidates in the general election of 1918 but only one was successful. She was Constance Markiewicz who represented the constituency of Dublin St. Patrick, but she could not take up her seat as she was in Holloway Prison. Of the seventeen, only one candidate stood in Wales – Millicent Mackenzie, a professor of education at Cardiff University, who was unsuccessful in her quest to become the Labour MP for the University of Wales seat.

The first female MP to sit in the House of Commons was Lady Nancy Astor who won a by-election and took over her husband's seat as Conservative MP for Plymouth in 1919 when he moved to the House of Lords. In 1929 Margaret Bondfield became the first female Cabinet member, serving as Minister of Labour in the second Labour Government until 1931.

SOURCE 27

Lady Nancy Astor, the first woman MP. She was an MP for 25 years and actively campaigned on women's issues

During the 1920s the number of women MPs gradually increased: 5 in 1922; 8 in 1923 and 14 in 1929, but they were still heavily outnumbered by 601 male MPs. In Wales the number of women candidates fighting in elections actually fell: 3 in 1922; one in 1923 and one in 1924. However, despite being few in numbers the women MPs in parliament did have an impact and they helped push forward legislation that brought more equal rights for women:

- 1919 Sex Disqualification Act – made it illegal to exclude women from jobs because of their sex;
- 1922 Married Women's Maintenance Act – provided women with an allowance;
- 1923 Matrimonial Causes Act – allowed women to divorce on the same grounds as men;
- 1923 Bastardy Act – increased maintenance payments for single mothers;
- 1925 Guardianship of Infants Act – gave mothers the same custody rights as fathers.

The general election of 1929 saw the election of Megan Lloyd George, the youngest child of David and Margaret Lloyd George, as the Liberal MP for Anglesey.

SOURCE 28

Megan Lloyd George addressing a crowd. She was the first female MP to secure a seat in Wales

At the age of 27 in 1929 she started a long political career, holding the Anglesey seat for the Liberal Party until 1951 and later becoming the Labour MP for Carmarthen from 1957 until her death in 1966.

The only other long-serving female MP during this period was Eleanor Rathbone who served as an Independent MP between 1929 and 1946.

Also in 1929 another Welsh woman was elected to parliament but for an English seat. Edith Picton Turbeville of Ewenny was elected as the Conservative MP for the Wrekin Division of Shropshire.

SOURCE 29

The 1929 election saw the great turning point for the hopes of Welsh women with the election of Megan Lloyd George, as Liberal MP for Anglesey. ... She was a lively, intelligent and fun loving woman, who was politically committed to a radical social agenda and she was also an ardent [passionate] nationalist. Her abilities were evident, but there can be no doubt that without her father's intervention she would never have been selected as Liberal candidate for the safe seat of Anglesey.

Deirdre Beddoe, 'Women and Politics in Twentieth Century Wales', which was the Annual Lecture to the Welsh Political Archive, 2004

In all, 36 women MPs were elected to the House of Commons in the inter-war years representing all three political parties. However, there were only 15 women in the Commons in any one parliament. During the 1930s, after an active two decades, feminist issues became less important to political parties, as the country now faced more acute problems such as unemployment and international peace.

TASKS

1. How important was the Representation of the People Act of 1928?

2. Describe the achievement of women MPs in the inter-war period.

3. Use Sources 28 and 29 and your own knowledge to explain why Megan Lloyd George is important in the political history of Wales.

This section provides guidance on how to answer Questions 2(c) and 3(c) from Unit 2. The question carries 8 marks in total but is sub-divided into 2 × 4-mark questions.

Questions 2(c) and 3(c) – the selection of knowledge and the understanding of key features

Explain why the votes for women campaign failed to achieve its aims before 1914.

[4 marks]

Tips on how to answer

- Aim to give a variety of reasons that are **well explained**.
- The **more reasons** you can mention, the better your chances of receiving the higher marks.
- Most importantly, these reasons need to be supported by **relevant factual detail.**
- Avoid generalised comments, as these will gain you low marks.
- Always support your statements with **examples**.
- Make sure the information you include is **directly relevant**. E.g. does it answer the question?

Response by candidate one

Women failed to gain the vote before 1914 because the government did not want to pass a law to give them the vote. Many MPs were against granting women the vote. They thought that a woman's role was that of a wife and mother and only men should be allowed to vote.

> Lack of factual support

Examiner's comment

A limited response that begins to address two factors – the reluctance of the government to grant the vote and existing male attitudes towards women and politics. However, the comments are generalised and lack specific factual support. The lack of detail confines the answer to Level One and it was awarded 2 marks.

Response by candidate two

The votes for women campaign failed to achieve its aims because many important MPs in the Liberal Government were against the idea, especially the Prime Minister Asquith. The government had many problems to deal with such as the Irish Question, the People's Budget and the passing of the Parliament Bill, which were seen as more important issues than votes for women. Also, the militant actions of the suffragettes such as window smashing and the attacks on private property lost the movement a lot of support from the public.

> 1st reason

> 2nd reason

> 3rd reason

Examiner's comment

The answer identifies a number of specific reasons and these are explained in some depth. Generalised comments have been avoided. There is a clear focus and a good depth of knowledge and understanding is demonstrated. It is worthy of maximum (4) marks.

Now you have a go

Explain why the First World War was important in helping women to obtain the vote in 1918.

[4 marks]

CHAPTER 8

HAVE WOMEN BENEFITTED FROM UK GOVERNMENT LEGISLATION SINCE THE 1960s?

Introduction

SOURCE 1

[In the 1960s] women were still second class citizens in the workplace, they had very few rights and could be sacked from their job simply because of the demands of pregnancy. Women were seen as mothers and housewives, but not business professionals.

Women of today are standing up and being counted. They work in the Army, on oilrigs, and have rebuilt damaged satellites in space. Being a woman no longer excludes you from doing any job carried out by a male. Young women enjoy having their own income and are choosing to fulfill their career ambitions instead of or before they consider having a family.

An article on 'Women in the workplace', which appeared in 2010 on the website: www.jobsite.co.uk

TASK

What does Source 1 tell you about how women have benefited from changes since the 1960s?

Over the past fifty years women have continued their fight to secure equality. Through the establishment of organizations like the Women's Liberation Movement they have actively campaigned for laws to end the disparity between the sexes and secure more choice and security for women both in the home and in the workplace.

THE GROWTH OF FEMINISM

The 1950s: the quiet years of the feminist movement

While the First World War contributed, in part, to women being granted the vote, the Second World War did not result in any significant political changes in the lives of women. Although women had participated in the war effort, after it was over they were encouraged to resume their traditional roles as wives and mothers. The 1950s saw a backlash against the 'new feminism' of the inter-war years. Popular forms of media such as films, the radio and women's magazines were influential in encouraging women to fulfil the role of 'wife and mother' and they gave a high profile to marriage and home life.

SOURCE 2

The 1950s marked the nadir [low point] of British feminism. In fact, what passed for 'feminism' then ... was a woolly set of aspirations [aims] based on women's 'special values', namely the promotion of world peace, democracy, good citizenship and partnership within marriage. The aim of the earlier generation of feminists to win equal rights was written off as old-fashioned, aggressive and irrelevant. ... In terms of Welsh feminism, there was a vacuum between the end of the war and the early 1970s, when the Women's Liberation Movement, the second feminist wave of the twentieth century, burst onto the scene.

Deirdre Beddoe, 'Women and Politics in Twentieth Century Wales', which was the Annual Lecture to the Welsh Political Archive (2004)

Many women felt that the campaigns of earlier years had been won, women's rights had been achieved and no major issues remained to be solved. As a result organized **feminism** declined during the 1950s.

However, though feminist issues did not gain a very high priority there were some important campaigns during the 1950s, particularly in the demand for equal pay and equal opportunities. Activists like the Labour MP Edith Summerskill fought for women's causes both in parliament and through pressure groups. In 1952 female teachers were granted equal pay and in 1954 parity of pay was granted in the civil service. The success of such campaigns was not the result of pressure from an organized women's movement but from a number of separate groups and organizations such as the Six Point Group, which campaigned for equal pay, the National Women's Citizens Associations, the Women's Cooperative Guild and the Women's Institute.

SOURCE 3

The Labour MP Edith Summerskill campaigned on feminist issues throughout the 1940s and 1950s, and held various Cabinet posts until her retirement from the Commons in 1961

SOURCE 4

it seemed clear that emancipation had failed: the number of women in Parliament had settled at a low level; the number of professional women had stabilized as a tiny minority; the pattern of female employment had emerged as underpaid, menial and supportive. The cage door had been opened but the canary had refused to fly out. The conclusion was that the cage door ought never to have been opened because canaries are made for captivity; the suggestion of an alternative had only confused and saddened them.

The feminist writer Germaine Greer commenting upon the limited progress made by women before the late 1960s in The Female Eunuch

TASKS

1. Explain why the 1950s is seen as the quiet years of the feminist movement.

2. Use Source 3 and your own knowledge to explain why women made some progress towards equality during the 1950s.

3. How useful is Source 2 to the historian studying the feminist movement before the late 1960s?

4. Study Source 4. What did Germaine Greer mean by saying that 'the cage door had been opened and the canary had refused to fly out'?

Revival of feminism in the late 1960s and early 1970s

The feminist campaigns of the inter-war period are most often referred to as 'new feminism' and sometimes as 'first-wave feminism' and concentrated in the main upon obtaining equal suffrage. The movement that emerged in the late 1960s and 1970s is termed 'second-wave feminism' and called for equality of opportunities for women in such areas as education and employment, and a change in attitude towards women and their role in society. There was a growing feeling that women were treated as second-class citizens. More needed to be done to ensure that they obtained support from the state in terms of important issues such as contraception and divorce.

There were a number of reasons for this revival in feminism:

- The 1960s saw a growth in radicalism – e.g. women became involved in protests against nuclear weapons and inequalities like apartheid in South Africa;
- The growth in the number of university students coincided with them becoming more critical and politically active;
- Changing attitudes towards the relationship between the sexes, as more women came to feel that they were treated as second class citizens;
- The influence of feminist writers and campaigners like Germaine Greer who helped to provide academic support to the arguments;
- The influence of events elsewhere in the world – the civil rights movement in the USA; protests against the Vietnam war;
- European influence – during this period Britain was becoming closer to the European Economic Community (EEC), which it later joined in 1973 and therefore had to comply with the EEC Treaty legislation on equality;
- Attitude of the Labour government – during its first term in office Harold Wilson's Labour government issued a range of social reforms such as making homosexuality between consenting adults no longer an offence (1967) and the Abortion Act (1967).

The result was the development of a women's liberation movement, which saw women taking a more active role in political issues and pressing more forceful demands for equality between the sexes.

SOURCE 5

Each Member State shall during the first stage ensure and subsequently maintain the application of the principle that men and women should receive equal pay for equal work.

A Treaty Establishing the European Community as Amended by Subsequent Treaties, Rome, 25 March 1957, Part Three, Title VIII, Article 119

SOURCE 6

Protesters in London in 1967 demanding the legalisation of abortion

Germaine Greer (1939-)

- An Australian journalist and feminist writer;
- She did much to champion the cause of feminism in the late twentieth century;
- In 1970 she wrote *The Female Eunuch*, a book that became one of the key works of the feminist movement of the 1970s;
- She argued that women should stand up for their rights and play an equal role in society.

TASKS

1. What does Source 6 show you about the involvement of women in politics in the late 1960s?

2. Explain why feminism was revived in the late 1960s.

3. Study Source 5. How did Britain's application to join the EEC help the campaign by women for equality?

4. Research the career of Germaine Greer. Why is she important in the campaign for women's liberation from the 1970s onwards?

The Women's Liberation Movement

Local women's groups were started all over the country and by 1969 there were over 70 women's liberation groups in London alone. They aimed to draw attention to how widespread discrimination against women was. They questioned the traditional male assumptions that saw women as the homemakers who would leave work once they married and give up their independence on the birth of any children. The members of such groups spoke about a 'consciousness rising' as they aimed to make women aware of their own ideas about themselves and their roles in society.

In 1970 the various branches of the women's liberation movement, or 'women's lib' as it increasingly became known, came together at a national conference to plan an overall programme of action. They came up with four key demands:

SOURCE 7

The resurgence of the women's movement in the late 1960s heralded a new assault on the many ways in which successive generations of women have been confined within the 'cage' of domesticity and low esteem at home and at work.

G. Braybon & P. Summerfield, Out of the Cage: Women's Experiences in Two World Wars *(1987), page 287*

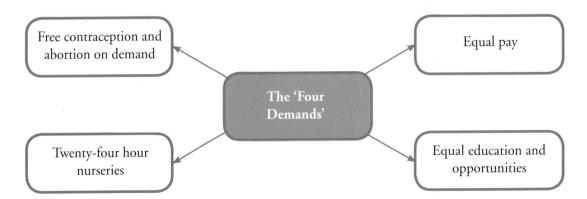

Free contraception and abortion on demand

Equal pay

The 'Four Demands'

Twenty-four hour nurseries

Equal education and opportunities

The conference launched the women's liberation movement on the national scene. It was a vehicle through which radical feminist issues could be discussed and their message delivered to the public at large. The movement's demands were printed on banners and on a petition handed to the Prime Minister on 6 March 1971 when 4,000 marched through London on the movement's first 'International Women's Day' march.

A consequence of the movement was the establishment of feminist magazines, which provided alternatives to traditional women's magazines of the time that dwelled on issues such as beauty, romance and domestic life. Magazines like *Shrew*, first published in 1969, and *Spare Rib*, which first appeared in 1972, highlighted feminist issues. In its early years *Spare Rib* sold around 20,000 copies per month but some newsagents, like W. H. Smith, refused to stock it because of its radical nature. In 1973 the Virago Press was set up to publish books by women writers and it did much to further the feminist cause.

One of the most headline-grabbing actions of the Women's Liberation Movement was the demonstration it staged in November 1970 at the Miss World Competition held at the Royal Albert Hall in London. Demonstrators carried placards reading: *'Miss-fortune demands equal pay for women, Miss-conception demands free abortion for all women, Miss-placed demands a place outside the home'*. Their slogan was: *'We're not beautiful, we're not ugly, we're angry.'* Some demonstrators were arrested and five were later put on trial for throwing flour bombs, tomatoes and stink bombs. The event gained widespread newspaper and television coverage and did much to raise the profile of the campaign for women's rights.

A demonstration outside the Royal Albert Hall in November 1970 protesting against the Miss World Competition. Ref: http://www.nickelinthemachine.com/

In attempting to sum up the achievements of the feminist movement during the 1970s the BBC Radio 4 programme *Woman's Hour* concluded:

This was the decade of feminism. Landmark books like Germaine Greer's *The Female Eunuch* and Kate Millet's *Sexual Politics* sold in their millions. Magazines like *Ms* and *Spare Rib* increasingly found their way into women's homes and the feminist publishers Virago was launched.

Taken from the BBC Radio 4 website http://www.bbc.co.uk/ radio4/womanshour/timeline/keyevents_print.shtml?1970

TASKS

1. What does Source 8 show you about the reaction of the Women's Liberation Movement to the Miss World Competition held in 1970?

2. How important were radical female magazines and a female publishing press to the growth of the Women's Liberation Movement? You may wish to use Source 9 for information.

3. Explain why the first national conference of the Women's Liberation Movement held in 1970 was important.

4. How useful is Source 9 to an historian studying the impact of the Women's Liberation Movement?

1975-85: The 'Decade for Women'

By the mid-1970s the struggle for women's rights had become an issue in many countries around the world. To help raise the profile of such issues 1975 was designated International Women's Year and the UN followed this by declaring the years 1975-85 the United Nations Decade for Women.

Within the UK women's liberation groups were active in campaigning for a variety of causes such as greater control over the process of childbirth and the increased representation of women in public life. They also campaigned against cuts in health and social services, against pornography and its exploitation of women, and against the allocation of senior posts to men. The campaigns operated on both a national and a regional level, some of the campaigns being specific to certain localities.

During this period the Women's Liberation Movement became politicized, examples being:

- **1975 Wages for Housework Campaign**
  In 1972 the American feminist Selma James founded the International Wages for Housework Campaign. In 1975 a demonstration was held in London by Women's Liberation activists who demanded money from the government for unwaged work in the home.

- **1976 Women's Peace Movement (later Peace People)**
  This was started in Ulster in August 1976 to try and bring an end to the religious troubles in Northern Ireland. In the months that followed up to 20,000 Catholics and Protestants took to the streets in huge rallies, calling for an end to the violence. A march in London attracted a crowd of 30,000. The founders, Betty Williams and Mairead Corrigan Maguire were awarded the Nobel Peace Prize in 1977.

- **1981-2000 Greenham Common Women's Peace Camp**
  The Peace Camp was established in September 1981 by a Cardiff group – 'Women for Life on Earth' who wanted to protest against American nuclear missiles being sited at RAF Greenham Common in Berkshire. Their numbers quickly grew and at a rally held in December 1982 30,000 women joined hands around the base at the 'Embrace the Base' event.

On that chilly December day the Greenham Women had invited all-comers to join them to 'Embrace the base': to face the potential threat of nuclear destruction with a peaceful, loving embrace. It was a call-to-arms I, then aged 19, could not resist. And so I joined a twelve-mile-long chain of mostly women 30,000 strong. I stood hand in hand with them around the perimeter fence, singing, chanting, protesting. It was in this spirit that the Peace Camp was womanned for 19 years.

The memories of Jane Tomlinson who took part in the 'Embrace the Base' demonstration in December 1982

While much of the protest was peaceful there were some occasions during the camp's nineteen-year history when the wire of the perimeter was cut and protestors entered the camp to daub peace slogans on huts and equipment. Such actions did result in arrests and prosecutions. The Camp closed in the year 2000 following the removal of the last nuclear missiles.

Women holding hands around RAF Greenham Common in December 1982

- **1984-85 Women's support for the Miners' Strike**
  In March 1984 the National Union of Mineworkers (NUM) began a strike against pit closures that was to last for nearly a year. Many women's groups such as the national group Women Against Pit Closures (WAPC) as well as regional groups such as the Maerdy Women's Support Group, the North

Staffordshire Miners Wives Action Group and the Aylesham Miners Wives Support Group, became active in support of the miners. These women played an important role in the strike, raising money to help support the miners and their families.

By the mid-1980s there were some 300 feminist groups in Britain with some 20,000 activists. Such groups had been demonstrating in support of a range of issues such as the right for equal pay and equal opportunities, the right to choose abortion and protests against nuclear bases.

However, it would be wrong to assume that feminist demands were welcomed by all women. Many women were content with their lifestyle and some even objected to the radical actions of the feminists who publicly burned their bras and used such newly coined phrases as 'sexism' and 'male chauvinist pig'. A counter-argument was that feminists who lobbied for greater access to male occupations based their arguments on high profile jobs such as doctors, lawyers, and university professors, ignoring the fact that for every one such job there were at least ten that consisted of working on an assembly line, driving a lorry or bus, or clerking in a store. Many women did not want these jobs.

SOURCE 12

An important source of support for the miners came from within their own communities, particularly from the women. Locally they set up Women's Action Groups through which they organised soup kitchens, distributed food parcels and organised Christmas appeals for miners' families. The women also actively joined picket lines, were involved in confrontations with the police and travelled the country speaking at political meetings. Nationally, women organised the 'Women Against Pit Closures' conference and, following the 'National Women Against Pit Closures' rally in London on 11th August 1984, handed a petition to the Queen.

From the social history website: www.archiveshub.ac.uk, set up by the University of Manchester (2000)

SOURCE 14

One mistake made by Women's Lib, it seems, has been to show open contempt for "sisters" who actually like to stay at home. ... Many busy housewives find their lives a good deal more varied than their husbands' working day. And they *enjoy* cooking, needlework and other pursuits derided by the feminists.
    Women's Lib may also have erred in ignoring the fact that men, too, often have boring and unfulfilling jobs.

An extract from The Punch Book of WOMEN, *edited by William Davis, 1973*

SOURCE 13

A march by the Maerdy Women's Support Group at the time of the miners' strike in 1984, flying their banner and slogan 'Your fight is our fight'

TASKS

1. What does Source 11 tell you about the growth of the Women's Liberation Movement by the 1980s?

2. Describe examples of how the Women's Liberation Movement became politically active during the 1970s and 1980s.

3. Use Sources 12 and 13 and your own knowledge to explain why women played an important role in the Miners' Strike of 1984-85.

4. Did all women support the feminist demands put forward by the Women's Liberation Movement? You may wish to use Source 14 for information.

MOVES TOWARDS EQUALITY

Government legislation

In the late 1960s and the 1970s feminist groups focused their struggle on the fight to abolish discrimination and secure equal rights and opportunities in all aspects of life. Increasingly politicians found themselves under pressure from organizations such as Women's Lib to introduce laws to bring about more equality between the sexes and protect the rights of women. As a result several key pieces of legislation were passed during this time.

The Abortion Act (1967)

This Act was passed in October 1967 as a result of a private member's bill introduced by David Steel, but it did have the backing of the Labour government. The issue of abortion is controversial and was especially so in the 1960s and while there was strong support from feminist groups for such a bill there was equally strong opposition, especially from religious groups. MPs were given a free vote and they voted in favour.

When the law came into effect in April 1968 it made abortion legal in the UK and it could be carried out under the NHS within 28 weeks of conception if two doctors were satisfied that the operation was necessary on medical or psychological grounds. As with the introduction of the contraceptive pill in 1961 it now gave women more control over their lives.

In 1975 the National Abortion Campaign (NAC) was set up to protest against any changes to the 1967 Act and to campaign for its improvement.

SOURCE 15

Badges worn by women during the late 1970s as part of the National Abortion Campaign

The Divorce Reform Act (1969)

This Act was again the result of a private member's bill and came into effect in 1971. It was intended to make divorce fairer for women. It allowed a couple to divorce on the grounds of adultery, cruelty, desertion, or by mutual consent (after two years apart), or after five years if only one person wanted a divorce.

The Equal Pay Act (1970)

During the 1960s women's groups had attempted to draw attention to the fact that employers, who paid them lower wages than men for doing the same job, often exploited women. This discrimination was highlighted during the summer of 1968 when 850 women sewing-machinists walked out of the Ford Motor Co. Factory at Dagenham in Essex in protest over their unequal treatment. Their three-week strike was only ended after the Secretary of State for Employment, Barbara Castle, met with the women and took up their cause to get them back to work. As a result they were awarded a pay increase.

SOURCE 16

The Ford sewing machinists strike of 1968 was a landmark labour-relations dispute in the United Kingdom. It ultimately led to the passing of the Equal Pay Act 1970, the first legislation in the UK aimed at ending pay discrimination between men and women.

... Spurred on by their example, women trades unionists founded the National Joint Action Campaign Committee for Women's Equal Rights (NJACCWER), which held an 'equal pay demonstration' attended by 1,000 people in Trafalgar Square on 18 May, 1969.

Taken from an article 'Ford sewing machinists strike of 1968' on an internet site

The result of such pressure was the passing of the Equal Pay Act in 1970, which came into force in 1975. It prohibited inequality of treatment between men and women in terms of pay and conditions of employment.

Women strikers at the Ford Motor Co. factory in Dagenham, Essex, in June 1968. A film dramatisation of the strike, Made in Dagenham, *was released in 2010*

The Employment Protection Act (1975)

This was an important step forward as it granted working women the right to maternity leave and pay. Mothers who had been with their employers for at least two years now had the right to their job back after childbirth. To qualify women had to return to full-time employment within 29 weeks of the birth and they were entitled to a small amount of paid leave (18 weeks at 90% of earnings).

The Sex Discrimination Act (1975)

This Act gave legal protection to both men and women from discrimination on the grounds of gender. It made it illegal to discriminate against men or women in employment, housing, training, education, harassment and the provision of goods and services.

While this law made it illegal to discriminate solely on the grounds of gender it did little to force a change of attitude. It was now possible for women to fight injustices through the legal process but it did not mean that it would be easy to do so.

The Equal Opportunities Commission (1975)

This body was set up to ensure that the Equal Pay Act and the Sex Discrimination Act were implemented. In 2007 it was merged into a new body, The Equality and Human Rights Commission. Its function was to ensure equality and parity between the sexes as determined by government laws, and to take action if those laws had been broken.

Apart from these major laws, other legislation has been passed, which has helped women:

*   **Domestic Violence Act (1976)**: enables women to obtain a court order against their violent husband or partner;
*   **Human Fertilisation and Embryology Act (1990)**: this amended the 1967 Abortion Act and reduced the time limit for abortions from 28 to 24 weeks;
*   **Child Support Act (1991)**: this stated that absent parents now had a legal responsibility to contribute towards the upkeep of their child and it also set up the Child Support Agency;
*   **Family Law Act (1996)**: this established procedures to try and save marriages and give a structure to the divorce process.

TASKS

1.   What does Source 15 show you about the attitude of some women towards abortion?
2.   How useful is Source 16 to an historian studying the importance of the Ford Sewing Machinists' Strike of 1968?
3.   Explain why the Equal Opportunities Commission has been good for women.
4.   Which of the laws passed since 1967 have been most important in helping women to achieve equality? Give reasons for your answer.

The impact of legislation – have women achieved equality?

Since the late 1960s when the government began to pass a series of laws designed to achieve equality for women in law, considerable progress has been made in the drive to achieve parity with men. However, while laws can lay down rules and regulations they cannot change attitudes and opinions over night. This is a gradual process that is yielding results:

• Slowly the pay gap between men and women has narrowed, but direct parity has still not been achieved

• In education significant progress has been made and girls now perform better than boys at virtually every level.

• Women have increasingly taken on roles that historically have been seen as the preserves of men. In 1979 Margaret Thatcher became Britain's first female Prime Minister. In 1994 women were ordained as priests in the Church of England and in 1996 as priests in the Church of Wales.

• The number of female managers and executives has increased. Women managers are now getting promoted more quickly than their male counterparts and the proportion of women in management trebled from one in ten in 1994 to one in three in 2005. In 1992 Stella Rimington made the headlines by becoming the first female head of MI5, while that same year the MP Betty Boothroyd became the first woman to be elected Speaker of the House of Commons.

• The twenty-first century has witnessed increasing parity in social life through the emergence of 'ladette' culture. In 2001 the term 'ladette' made its first appearance in the Oxford Dictionary to describe young women who behave in a boisterous manner and engage in heavy drinking sessions. While ladette culture has embedded itself into British society it has also resulted in a backlash as the popular reality TV series *Ladette to Lady* has demonstrated. First viewed in 2005 the series aims to teach a group of ladettes how to behave in a lady-like manner.

SOURCE 20

Ladettes enjoying themselves

While women have made substantial progress on the road to achieving equality since the 1960s the campaign still continues, aiming to achieve absolute parity in all areas of society.

TASKS

1. What does Source 19 tell you about the progress made by women to achieve equality in management jobs?

2. Use Source 18 and your own knowledge to explain why, by 2010, it could be claimed that the pay gap between women and men had been reduced.

3. Describe ladette culture.

4. Has government legislation since the 1960s helped women to achieve full equality?

   You should give a two-sided answer to this question:

   - *discuss how government legislation has helped women to achieve equality;*

   - *discuss how full equality has not yet been achieved in all areas;*

   and give a judgement.

Examination practice

This section provides guidance on how to answer questions 2(d) and 3(d) from Unit 2. This is an extended answer question that provides a scaffold to help you structure your answer. The question carries 10 marks.

Questions 2(d) and 3(d) – using own knowledge to construct a two-sided essay

How successful have women been in their campaign for equality since the 1960s? Explain your answer fully.

[10 marks]

You should give a two-sided answer to this question:
- *discuss examples of success in the campaign for equality;*
- *discuss areas of less success, where equality is still to be achieved;*
and give a judgement.

Tips on how to answer

- You need to develop a **two-sided** answer that is balanced and well supported.

- You should start by discussing the **factor mentioned in the question**, using your factual knowledge to explain why this factor is important.

- You then need to consider the **counter-argument** by using your knowledge to examine other relevant factors.

- These points need to be discussed in some detail, starting a new paragraph for each point.

- Aim to link the paragraphs by using phrases such as 'other factors include', 'also important', 'in addition to', 'however'.

- **Avoid generalised comments** – the more specific your observations the higher the mark you will get, providing the factual information is relevant to the question.

- Conclude your answer with a **link back** to the question, making a judgement about the importance of the factor listed in the question when ranked against the other factors you have discussed.

- You should aim to write between one and two sides of a page.

Candidate response

Since the 1960s women have been successful in their campaign to achieve equality in certain areas such as equal pay, but less successful in other areas such as obtaining the top jobs in male dominated professions.

→ Introduction that links to the question

The rise of the Women's Liberation Movement in the 1970s did much to support and push forward the campaign for equality. Branches of Women's Lib were set up all over the country and became active in campaigning for issues such as a woman's right to abortion. The first national

→ Deals with key factor mentioned in the question

conference of the Women's Liberation Movement in 1970 came up with four demands, which included the right to equal pay and equal education, a call for 24-hour nurseries and the right to free contraception and abortion on demand. Through new magazines like 'Spare Rib' they drew attention to the inequalities that existed.

The Women's Liberation Movement carried out a number of high-profile protests and demonstrations such as that against the Miss World Competition in 1970. Another was the campaign against the placing of nuclear missiles at Greenham Common military base, and the establishment of a Women's Peace Movement in Northern Ireland.

During the 1970s women became increasingly active politically. The strike by female machinists at the Ford Car Factory at Dagenham in 1968 helped put pressure on the government to pass the Equal Pay Act in 1970. Through such pressure women's groups helped campaign for other laws such as the Sex Discrimination Act (1975) and the Employment Protection Act (1975), which granted women maternity leave and pay. The setting up of the Equal Opportunities Commission also helped women to fight against inequality in the workplace.

> Provides precise details to support the argument

However, such laws gave legal protection but could not change attitudes. Despite laws granting equal pay the pay gap in 2010 between women and men was still 10%. This gap has closed since the 1970s but it still exists. Despite the Sex Discrimination Act women are still finding it difficult to get the top jobs in professions dominated by men. In 1992 Stella Rimington became head of MI5 but such posts are rare. In 1994 women were ordained as priests in the Church of England but they have not yet been appointed bishops. Ladette culture allows younger women to compete with men in the club scene culture of the twenty first century.

> Begins the counter-argument. Using the term 'however' makes it clear that you are now looking at other factors

A number of laws have been passed since the 1960s granting women more equality with men. The gap has closed and is continuing to close but direct parity has not yet been achieved.

> Attempts a judgement linked back to the question

Examiner's comment

The answer addresses the question and provides relevant factual detail to illustrate and support observations. The answer is two-sided but lacks balance, as the counter-argument is not as detailed or as wide-ranging. The conclusion is also a little thin and could have been developed further. However, the depth of knowledge just pushed the answer into low Level 4. It was awarded 9 marks.

Was the growth of the Women's Liberation Movement the most important development that has helped women to achieve greater equality since the 1960s? Explain your answer fully.

[10 marks]

You should give a two-sided answer to this question:
- *discuss the importance of the Women's Liberation Movement;*
- *discuss other factors that have helped to bring greater equality for women;*
and give a judgement.

CHAPTER 9

HOW SUCCESSFUL HAVE WOMEN BEEN IN ACHIEVING IMPORTANT POLITICAL ROLES IN WALES AND ENGLAND?

Introduction

SOURCE 1

The female Labour MPs elected into office following the 1929 general election

TASK

What does Source 1 tell you about the representation of women in parliament in 1929?

Since gaining the vote in 1918 women have stood as candidates in every general election. Of those elected, some have achieved great parliamentary success, rising to become Cabinet Ministers and, in the case of Margaret Thatcher, even Prime Minister. However, until the late 1990s women MPs never amounted to more than 10% of the total number of MPs. Changes in **positive discrimination** enabled that figure to rise to 22% in the 2010 general election, but it is still far from achieving parity with men.

WOMEN IN THE UK PARLIAMENT

The first women MPs of the inter-war period

In 1918 women over 30 were granted the right to vote and ten years later, in 1928, the age limit was lowered to 21, giving women parity with men. Since 1918 women have been able to stand as candidates in parliamentary elections, but in the inter-war period the number of female MPs in any one parliament remained small. The highest percentage came in the general election of 1931, which saw the return of 15 female MPs, but even this figure amounted to just 2.4% of the total number of MPs in the House of Commons.

Such small numbers went against the initial concerns of some MPs who feared that by allowing women the right to stand for parliament the House of Commons would quickly be swamped by female members, as Source 2 illustrates.

An anti-suffrage cartoon by artist David Low. It appeared in 1929 shortly after the lowering of the voting age for women to 21

Several factors made it difficult for women to get elected:

- Politics was still viewed by many as the preserve of men and it was difficult for women to break into this male dominated world;
- Women found it difficult to be adopted as candidates by the main political parties;
- When they did find a seat, it was likely to be less winnable than those for which men had been selected;
- Westminster working hours are unsuitable for many women with families;
- Women may take career breaks to look after their children, which means they could be out of active politics for some time and find it difficult to return.

However, despite such obstacles, some women were successful in their efforts to become MPs: Countess de Markievicz in 1918, Lady Nancy Astor in 1919 and, in Wales, Megan Lloyd George in 1929 (Chapter 7).

The first three women Members of Parliament to take the oath were all elected for seats which had been held by their husbands. Lady Astor (Conservative) was joined in the House of Commons in 1921 by Margaret Wintringham (Liberal), who was returned for the marginal constituency of Louth even though, as a mark of respect to her dead husband, she had not spoken in public throughout her campaign.

In 1923, Mabel Hilton Philipson ... took over as the Conservative Member for Berwick-upon-Tweed after her husband (a National Liberal) had been unseated because of the fraudulent practices of his agent.

An extract from Women in the House of Commons, *a fact sheet produced by the House of Commons Information Office in June 2010*

Other notable successes were the election as MPs of Margaret Bondfield and Ellen Wilkinson, both of whom went on to hold important posts in Labour governments.

Margaret Bondfield (1873-1953)

The first woman to hold ministerial office was Margaret Bondfield who had been elected as the Labour MP for Northampton in 1923. An active trade unionist, she became the first female chairman of the Trades Union Congress (TUC) in 1923. In January 1924 she was appointed Under Secretary in the Ministry of Labour (the first women to be made a minister). In June 1929 she was appointed Minister of Labour and became the first female to sit in the Cabinet. She held this position until her parliamentary career came to an end in 1931 when she was defeated and Labour lost the General Election.

Ellen Wilkinson (1891-1947)

The daughter of a Manchester textile worker, Ellen's working class upbringing developed in her a strong interest in socialism. Before the First World War she was an organizer of the NUWSS and was elected as Labour MP for Middlesbrough East in 1924. She became known as 'Red Ellen', due both to the colour of her hair and her left-wing political views. She lost her seat in 1931 but in 1935 re-entered parliament as MP for Jarrow. She gained a reputation for her concern for the unemployed and in 1936 she helped organize the march of 200 unemployed workers from Jarrow to London. A sculpture, called 'The Spirit of Jarrow', was erected in 2001 to commemorate this event (see p.10). In the Labour government of 1945, Ellen Wilkinson was appointed Minister of Education and was responsible for the introduction of free milk for school children. She was the second female MP to hold a position in the Cabinet.

SOURCE 4

Election Year	Number of female MPs	% of MPs
1918	1	0.1%
1922	2	0.3%
1923	8	1.3%
1924	4	0.7%
1929	14	2.3%
1931	15	2.4%
1935	9	1.5%

Number of women MPs elected in General Elections held between 1918 and 1935

TASKS

1. What does Source 4 show you about the number of women MPs elected to parliament during the 1920s and 1930s?

2. How useful is Source 2 to an historian studying the impact of the first female MPs?

3. Use Source 3 and your own knowledge to explain why women found it difficult to be elected MPs.

4. Describe the political achievements of either (a) Margaret Bondfield or (b) Ellen Wilkinson.

Women MPs in the post-war decades, 1945-85

The period after the Second World War saw an increase in the number of women being elected MPs, rising substantially from just 9 MPs following the 1935 General Election to 24 following the landslide Labour victory in the 1945 election. However, despite this rise the figure of 20+ women MPs remained relatively constant in all the elections throughout the 1950s through to the early 1980s, apart from the elections held in 1951 and 1979 when the number of women MPs actually fell below twenty. Throughout these four decades, despite averaging around 51% of the UK population, women MPs never made up more than 4.6% of the members of the House of Commons.

While women were poorly represented within the House of Commons this did not prevent them from being effective and active members. In 1959 Margaret Thatcher introduced a private member's bill to extend the rights of the public and press to be present at meetings of local authorities and other public bodies. When the Public Bodies (Admission to Meetings) Act became law in 1960 it made history, being the first act sponsored through parliament by a female MP in the Commons and a female peer in the Lords (Baroness Elliot).

Margaret Thatcher went on to achieve some other notable firsts for women MPs, becoming the first female leader of the Conservative Party in 1975 and the first female to be elected Prime Minister in 1979.

SOURCE 5

The Conservative victory at the 1979 General Election brought about another "first" when the Rt Hon Margaret Thatcher became the first British woman Prime Minister having led the Conservative Party since February 1975. However, at the same time, the 1979 election returned the lowest number of women MPs for nearly thirty years [just 19]. Only one other woman held Cabinet office during the time that Margaret Thatcher was Prime Minister. This was Baroness Young, who was Lord Privy Seal and Leader of the House of Lords in 1982-83.

An extract from Women in the House of Commons, *a fact sheet produced by the House of Commons Information Office in June 2010*

SOURCE 6

Parliamentary firsts for women

1918	MP elected (Countess Constance de Markievicz)
1919	MP to take seat (Nancy Astor)
1924	Minister (Margaret Bondfield)
1929	Cabinet Minister (Margaret Bondfield)
1958	Life Peers (Lady Reading & Baroness Wooton)
1964	Parliamentary Whip – Commons (Harriet Slater)
1965	Parliamentary Whip – Lords (Baroness Phillips)
1970	Deputy Speaker – (Betty Harvie Anderson)
1975	Leader of the Opposition (Margaret Thatcher)
1979	Prime Minister (Margaret Thatcher)
1981	Leader of the House of Lords (Baroness Young)
1992	Speaker of the House of Commons (Betty Boothroyd)
1997	Minister for Women (Joan Ruddock)
1998	Chief Whip (Ann Taylor)
2006	Foreign Secretary (Margaret Beckett)
2007	Home Secretary (Jacqui Smith)
2008	Chief Secretary to the Treasury (Yvette Cooper)
2010	Welsh Secretary (Cheryl Gillan)

A chart showing parliamentary 'firsts' for women MPs

While small in number, women MPs did have a significant impact upon national politics, none more so than Barbara Castle (1910-2002). Until her achievement was surpassed in 2007 by Gwyneth Dunwoody, she held the record as the longest continuously serving female MP. She represented Blackburn as its Labour MP from 1945 to 1979 and after leaving the Commons she went on to become the MEP for Greater Manchester from 1979 to 1989.

Barbara Castle held Cabinet posts in the Labour governments of Harold Wilson, serving successively as Minister for Overseas Development (1964-65), Minister for Transport (1965-68), Secretary for Employment and Productivity (1968-70), First Secretary of State (1968-70) and Secretary for Social Services (1974-76). While performing these jobs she was responsible for the introduction of the 70 mph speed limit and the breathalyser, equal pay laws and changes in child benefits. She had a distinguished political career.

SOURCE 7

Barbara's biggest achievement ... was the Equal Pay Act, introduced in 1970 ...

Barbara Castle was a hero to millions of British women. She inspired a new generation of women to become active in Labour politics .... Unlike Margaret Thatcher, who never appointed another woman to her cabinet, Barbara was a feminist who staunchly advanced the cause of women.

Comments made by the Labour MP Patricia Hewitt in The Guardian *in September 2008 concerning the achievements of Barbara Castle*

SOURCE 8

Irene Ward, Conservative

Barbara Castle, Labour

Gwyneth Dunwoody, Labour

Three female MPs who achieved notable 'firsts'

Another notable achievement was that of Irene Ward, who holds the record as the longest serving female MP in the House of Commons. She defeated the Labour MP Margaret Bondfield in the 1931 general election to become the new Conservative MP for Wallsend, a seat she held until 1945. In 1950 she was elected MP for Tynemouth and continued to represent that constituency until 1974.

TASKS

1. What does Source 6 tell you about the achievement of women in politics?

2. Use Source 7 and your own knowledge to explain why Barbara Castle was regarded as 'a hero to millions of British women'.

3. How successful were women MPs in obtaining parliamentary posts in the period 1945-1985?

Welsh women in parliament in the post-war decades, 1945-85

During the brief period 1950-51 Wales had three women MPs in Westminster, a situation that was not repeated until the 1990s. Megan Lloyd George represented Anglesey until 1951 and then Carmarthen between 1957 and 1966 as its Labour MP. In 1950 Eirene White was elected as Labour MP for East Flintshire, a position she held until 1970, before going to the House of Lords. Also in 1950 Dorothy Rees, a doctor's daughter, was elected Labour MP for Barry, before losing her seat to a Conservative in 1951.

Eirene White after winning the East Flintshire seat for the first time in the 1950 general election

The defeat of Dorothy Rees in 1951, the death of Lady Megan in 1966 and Eirene White's move to the House of Lords meant that after 1970 Wales did not have a single woman MP. This situation lasted for fourteen years, from 1970 to 1984. This was the low point in the representation of Wales by females.

In 1984 the Labour candidate, Ann Clwyd, won a by-election in the Cynon Valley. Between 1984 and 1997 she was the only female MP to hold a seat in Wales and in the words of the historian Deirdre Beddoe 'in those years she was, in effect, MP for women in Wales.'

Better success has been achieved in the European Parliament. In the first European Election of 1979 women won two of the four Welsh seats. Beata Brookes won the North Wales seat for the Conservatives and held it until 1989. Ann Clwyd, prior to going to Westminster, was elected as the MEP for Mid and West Wales in 1979, holding the seat until 1984.

[Eirene White] was elected Labour MP for East Flint in 1950, one of the first female MPs in Wales. ...

When Labour came to power under Harold Wilson in 1964, ... [she] became parliamentary under-secretary at the Colonial Office, in 1966 Minister of State for Foreign Affairs and in 1967 Minister of State at the Welsh Office for three years. White managed to hang on to her marginal constituency for 20 years, at one election by just 72 votes. ...

In 1970, she retired from the House of Commons and was made a life peer as Baroness White, of Rhymney in the County of Monmouth. ... She was Deputy Speaker of the House of Lords from 1979 to 1989.

An obituary notice that appeared on an internet site following the death of Eirene White, aged 90, in December 1999

TASKS

1. What does Source 9 tell you about the involvement of women in Welsh politics?

2. Why is the election of Ann Clwyd in 1984 so important in Welsh political history?

3. Describe the career and achievements of Eirene White. You may wish to use Source 10 for information.

Changes in female representation in Westminster since 1985

A key turning point in the number of women MPs sitting in the Commons came in the 1987 general election when their number nearly doubled to 41 from the 23 elected in 1983. In that year Diane Abbott became the first black woman to become an MP, representing Hackney North and Stoke Newington. Since 1987 the figure has continued to rise with each successive general election.

Significant increases occurred during the 1990s when the figure of 60 women MPs elected in 1992 doubled to 120 in the 1997 general election. Of these 120 MPs, 101 were Labour compared with just 13 Conservatives. This election saw the Labour Party's landslide victory under its new leader Tony Blair and as a result these new female Labour MPs were given the nickname 'Blair Babes'.

Prime Minister Tony Blair standing with the female Labour MPs elected into parliament in 1997. They became known as the 'Blair Babes'

Election Year	Number of female MPs	% of MPs
1983	23	3.5%
1987	41	6.3%
1992	60	9.2%
1997	120	18.2%
2001	118	17.9%
2005	128	19.8%
2010	143	22%

Number of women MPs elected in General Elections held between 1983 and 2010

In 2005 128 women MPs were returned to the House of Commons, a figure that represented nearly 20% of all MPs. In 2010 that figure rose to 22%, with 143 women MPs taking their seats in the Commons.

A number of reasons explain the rise in the number of female MPs since the late 1990s:
- The use by the Labour Party of all-women shortlists since the 1997 general election;
- The Sex Discrimination (Election Candidates) Act (2002) legalised all-women short lists as a method of selection;
- In 2005 David Cameron introduced a priority list (the 'A List') for the top 100 Conservative target seats, which set a target for women MPs. From 2006 constituency associations had to draw up shortlists where at least half the candidates were women.

This rise in the number of female MPs led to a corresponding increase in the number of women holding Cabinet posts in both the Blair and Brown Labour governments. In Blair's first Cabinet in 1997 five women held Ministerial posts:

- Ann Taylor: Leader of the House of Commons & Lord President of the Council (1997-98)
- Harriet Harman: Minister for Women & Secretary of State for Social Security (1997-98)
- Mo Mowlam: Secretary of State for Northern Ireland (1997-99)
- Claire Short: Secretary of State for International Development (1997-2003)
- Margaret Beckett: President of the Board of Trade (1997-98)

Women continued to hold Cabinet and ministerial posts in the Blair governments of 2001 and 2005, and in that of his successor Gordon Brown. In the Coalition Cabinet formed by David Cameron following the 2010 general election four of the 23 Cabinet posts were given to women. Theresa May was appointed Home Secretary, Cheryl Gillan became the first woman to be appointed Welsh Secretary and Lady Warsi, Minister without Portfolio, became the first Muslim woman to serve in the Cabinet. Yet, despite these appointments, women are still under-represented in both the Cabinet, the government and in parliament.

There are not enough women in the coalition government, according to the new Equalities Minister [the Liberal Democrat MP Lynne Featherstone] who told David Cameron to do more to promote female politicians. ...

Miss Featherstone admitted that her party had a long way to go on promoting women. She said: "The issue is how do you get women through the ranks of Parliament to those positions where they are then in a position to be in the Cabinet?"

Referring to the figures behind the coalition deal, she said: "If you look at the negotiating teams they were male and pale. I think that is an issue."

Comments made by Lynne Featherstone, a Liberal-Democrat MP, following the creation of the Coalition Government in May 2010. They were reported in The Telegraph *newspaper on 15 May 2010*

TASKS

1. Who were the 'Blair Babes'?

2. What does Source 12 tell you about the number of women MPs elected to parliament between 1983 and 2010?

3. Explain why the number of women MPs has risen sharply since the 1990s.

4. What is the main message about female representation put forward by Lynne Featherstone in Source 13? Do you agree with her views?

THE WELSH GOVERNMENT

The formation of the National Assembly for Wales

In September 1997 a referendum on devolution resulted in a 50.3% vote in favour of Wales having its own assembly. The Government of Wales Act (1998) set up the National Assembly for Wales, which now sits in The Senedd building in Cardiff Bay. The Assembly is made up of 60 Assembly Members (AMs) – 40 to represent constituencies and 20 by the additional member system. It is run through a Cabinet of ten ministers and between 2000 and 2009 the First Minister was Rhodri Morgan followed by the present incumbent Carwyn Jones.

Elections to the Assembly are held every four years. Since it was opened in 1999 there have been four Assembly elections, which were held in 1999, 2003, 2007 and 2011. Each has resulted in a Labour majority.

The Senedd building of the National Assembly of Wales, which was opened in 2006

Attempts to ensure equality of representation

One hope of devolution was that it would bring with it a new style of politics, one that was more representative of society. To a great extent this has been achieved in Wales through some of the main political parties adopting methods of selecting candidates that encouraged greater female participation.

In the 1999 election Welsh Labour used a method of 'twinning' or pairing constituencies to ensure equal numbers of men and women Labour candidates. Plaid Cymru took the step of ensuring that women topped each list for the 20 regional seats. As a result of such measures 40% of all the AMs elected were women. In the 2003 election this figure rose to 50% but fell back slightly to 46.7% in the 2005 election. These election results have served to make Wales the most female representative parliament in the world.

SOURCE 15

One of the success stories of post-devolution Wales was the exceptionally high level of representation achieved by women in the National Assembly. Following the elections of May 2003, women constituted 50 per cent of the membership of the Assembly, the highest proportion of women's representation in the world.

Geraint H. Jenkins, historian, writing in
A Concise History of Wales (2007)

SOURCE 16

We understand that it is the only legislature in the world that is perfectly balanced between men and women. ... the people of Wales have every right to be proud of having set that new world record.

Statement made by the First Minister, Rhodri
Morgan, following the 2003 elections to the
National Assembly for Wales

SOURCE 17

Political Party	Women AMs	Total AMs	% Women
Labour	19	30	63.3
Plaid Cymru	6	12	50.0
Liberal Democrats	3	6	50.0
Conservatives	2	11	18.2
Independent		1	0.0
Total	30	60	50.0

Women's representation in the 2003 National Assembly for Wales election

Women in the Welsh Government

Since its creation in 1999 women have played an important role in the National Assembly. Within the Cabinet the number of female AMs holding Ministerial posts has ranged between 6 and 4 members, providing them with a key voice in the decision making process. Some of the women in the Cabinet have held positions within it since 1999. Among them is Jane Davidson, the AM for Pontypridd since 1999 who has held three ministerial roles including that of Deputy Presiding Officer. Edwina Hart, the AM for Gower, has held four ministerial posts since 1999 as has Jane Hutt the AM for the Vale of Glamorgan. Elin Jones, the Plaid Cymru AM for Ceredigion, held various shadow ministerial posts before entering the Cabinet in the 'One Wales Government' in 2007 as the Minister of Rural Affairs.

Women have also risen to high positions within the political parties of Wales. In December 2008 Kirsty Williams became the leader of the Liberal Democrat Party in Wales, becoming the first female leader of a political party in Wales. In 2012 Leane Wood was elected leader of Plaid Cymru.

We should let it sink in that Wales – a country which throughout the twentieth century had a truly appalling record of female representation – now tops the world league table with 50 per cent of women in our National Assembly. The Assembly Government Cabinet has a majority of female members.
There has been a revolution in Welsh politics.

Comments made upon the 2003 election results to the National Assembly by the feminist historian Deirdre Beddoe in her lecture 'Women and Politics in Twentieth Century Wales', the Annual Lecture to the Welsh Political Archive in 2004

TASKS

1. What do Sources 15 and 16 tell you about the success of women AMs in the National Assembly for Wales?

2. Explain why the election of women AMs to the National Assembly for Wales has been so successful.

3. Use Source 17 and your own knowledge to explain why the 2003 election for the National Assembly is important in the history of female involvement in politics.

4. How successful have women AMs been in obtaining cabinet posts? You may wish to use Source 18 for information.

THE ACHIEVEMENTS OF WOMEN IN MODERN POLITICAL LIFE

Despite being heavily outnumbered by their male counterparts, women MPs have risen to occupy some of the top posts in modern political life. Within the House of Lords three noticeable achievements have been:

- **Baroness Young** – in 1981 she became the first female Leader of the House of Lords, a post she held until 1983. She was responsible for organizing the business of the Lords and represented the House of Lords on formal occasions.
- **Baroness Hale of Richmond** – she was appointed a Law Lord in 2004, which made her the most senior female judge in the UK.
- **Baroness Hayman** – she was appointed the first ever Lord Speaker, a post that replaced that of Lord Chancellor in 2006.

Within the last thirty years some women MPs in the House of Commons have made significant advances in the quest to obtain the top posts or achieve significant firsts:

Caroline Lucas – born in Malvern, Worcestershire, Caroline Lucas was a Green Party Member of the European Parliament (MEP) from 1999 to 2010. She was leader of the Green Party of England and Wales between 2008 and 2012 and has been voted the UKs 'Most Ethical Politician' three times by readers of the *Observer* newspaper. In 2010 she was elected as the Green Party Member of Parliament for Brighton Pavilion, making her the only Green Party MP in the House of Commons.

Margaret Thatcher – in 1979 she became Britain's first female prime minister and went on to become the longest serving prime minister of the twentieth century, holding office for 11 years and 209 days.

The daughter of a shopkeeper and mayor of Grantham in Lincolnshire, Margaret became interested in politics whilst a student at Oxford University. In 1959 she was elected Conservative MP for Finchley and in 1970 was appointed Education Secretary in the government of Edward Heath. In 1975 she challenged and defeated Heath for the Party leadership, to become the first female to lead a political party. She developed a radical right-wing philosophy that became known as 'Thatcherism'. In 1979 the Conservatives won the general election and she became the UK's first female prime minister.

Margaret Thatcher dominated UK politics throughout the 1980s, winning landslide election victories in 1983 and 1987. Her forceful style of leadership and policies won her the nickname 'The Iron Lady'. She led the country through the Falklands War of 1982 and carried out a radical programme of privatisation and deregulation. She clashed with the trade unions and refused to back down in the Miners' Strike of 1984-85 or from the introduction of the poll tax. While she was liked by many she also had many enemies and in December 1990 she was forced to resign when her own Cabinet turned against her. Her successor, John Major, made her a life peer in 1992.

SOURCE 19

As Prime Minister she became the most important commoner in the land. Some saw her elections as a victory for feminism. She is both wife and mother and still succeeded in pursuing a highly successful career. Others claimed that she 'owed nothing to feminism' and was the 'best man' to lead the Conservative government. It has been said that she herself was very aware of the disadvantage of being a woman. Yet, at times, she used her femininity.

W. Gareth Evans, The Role and Changing Status of Women in the Twentieth Century, *(2000), p. 100*

Betty Boothroyd – in 1992 she became the first female to be appointed Speaker of the House of Commons, a post she held for 8 years until her retirement in 2000.

The daughter of a textiles worker from Dewsbury in the West Riding of Yorkshire, Betty Boothroyd grew up during the harsh years of the Depression. At the age of 16 she joined the Labour League of Youth and obtained a job as a secretary. After moving to London she became the secretary to two MPs, one of whom was Barbara Castle, and this developed further her interest in politics. She contested several elections before being elected MP for West Bromwich in the 1973 general election. In 1974 she became the first woman to be appointed Labour Whip.

She established a reputation of being the 'housewives' champion' and in 1976 she introduced a Consumer Protection Bill to deal with rising prices. During the Thatcher era she was an active opposition backbencher and in 1992 made history by being appointed Speaker. She never married, dedicating her life to politics and upon her retirement in 2000 she made the comment 'If I had married, I doubt I would have become Speaker.'

Harriet Harman

Born in London, Harriet Harman was elected Labour MP for Peckham in 1982, a position she retained in the 2010 general election, which made her the longest serving female MP in the Commons. In her distinguished political career she has held a number of ministerial positions, the first being Secretary of State for Social Security (1997-98) and Minister for Women (1997-98). She was Leader of the House of Commons (2007-10) and following the resignation of Gordon Brown she became Acting Leader of the Labour Party for five months in 2010. Under the new leadership of Ed Milliband she was appointed Shadow Secretary of State for International Development.

Ann Clwyd

Brought up in Pentre Halkyn in Flintshire, Ann Clwyd obtained a degree from the University College of Wales in Bangor before embarking upon a career as a journalist. Between 1964-79 she served as Welsh correspondent for the *Guardian* and *Observer* newspapers. After several unsuccessful attempts as a Labour candidate in general elections, she was elected as MEP for Mid and West Wales in 1979. She remained MEP until 1984 when she was elected as MP for Cynon Valley, becoming the first woman to sit for a Welsh valleys constituency.

She held various posts in the Shadow Labour Cabinet including that of Shadow Secretary of State for Overseas Development (1989-92) and Shadow Secretary of State for Wales (1992). In 2003 Tony Blair made her Special Envoy on Human Rights in Iraq in the run-up to the Iraq War. Between 2005-2006 she was Chair of the Parliamentary Labour Party and is currently Wales' longest serving female MP.

Since the 1980s women have be represented more in the political process and have achieved high office in parliamentary government – at Westminster, at the National Assembly and at the local level in terms of councillors in local government.

SOURCE 20

I am pleased to see all the women in the House, because I know from personal experience how difficult it has been for women to be elected. I was the only woman from Wales here for 14 years ... It was a long fight; there had been only three women MPs from Wales before I was elected in 1984, two of whom were daughters of famous men. One was Lloyd George's daughter, and the other was the daughter of the then Deputy Chief Secretary to the Treasury. The third was Dorothy Rees, who was unfortunately defeated after one year. That is why some of us speak with considerable feeling about the difficulties of getting here.

I was elected in competition with a lot of other people, but I know that if it had not been for all-women shortlists, I would probably not have been joined by other women from Wales.

Part of a speech made by Ann Clwyd in a debate on International Women's Day in the House of Commons on 6 March 2008. She is talking about how difficult it is for women to become MPs (Hansard, HC Deb 6 March 2008, column 1950)

TASKS

1. What does Source 19 tell you about the personality of Margaret Thatcher?

2. Describe the career and political achievements of either (a) Betty Boothroyd or (b) Ann Clwyd.

3. How far does Source 20 support the view that women in Wales have always found it difficult to be elected to parliament?

4. How successful have women been in political life from 1900 to the present day? Explain your answer fully.

   You should give a two-sided answer to this question:
   - *discuss the success achieved by women in political life;*
   - *discuss the lack of success;*
   and then give a judgement.

Examination practice

Here is an opportunity for you to practise some of the questions that have been explained in previous chapters.

SECTION A

These questions are taken from Section A of the examination and form an enquiry into the changing role of women in political life in Wales and England. The questions test your source evaluation skills and are worth 25 marks in total.

Question 1(a) – comprehension of a visual source

SOURCE A

A crowd assembled in Trafalgar Square to hear speakers demanding equal rights for men and women, 6 March 1970

(a) What does Source A show you about the Women's Liberation Movement?

[2 marks]

- *Remember to pick out at least two facts from the picture.*
- *You must also make use of the information provided in the caption.*
- *For further guidance, see page 59.*

Question 1(b) – comprehension of a source and the recall of own knowledge

SOURCE B

In politics there were permanent changes. In 1918 women aged 30 and over received the vote ... As a result, some 8 million women were eligible [able] to vote, and women were also eligible [able] to become Members of Parliament.

From Contemporary Britain 1914-1979, *Robert Pearce*

(b)   Use the information in Source B and your own knowledge to explain why the period from 1918 to 1928 was important for women in politics.

[4 marks]

- *You will need to pick out at least two facts from the source and explain them in your own words.*
- *You must demonstrate your knowledge of this topic by providing at least one additional factor not mentioned in the source.*
- *For further guidance, see page 13.*

Question 1(c) – extent of support for a viewpoint

SOURCE C

Election Year	Number of women MPs elected	% of total MPs
1945	24	3.8%
1950	21	3.4%
1951	17	2.7%
1955	24	3.8%
1959	25	4.0%
1964	29	4.6%
1966	26	4.1%
1970	26	4.1%
1974 (Feb)	23	3.6%
1974 (Oct)	27	4.3%
1979	19	3.0%
1983	23	3.5%

The number of women MPs elected in General Elections held between 1945 and 1985. Taken from the House of Commons fact sheet 'Women in the House of Commons' (2009)

(c)   How far does Source C support the view that women were not very successful at being elected MPs between 1945 and 1985?

[5 marks]

- *You must pick out a range of factors from both the source and the caption, linking them to your own knowledge.*
- *Remember to give a reasoned judgement that targets the question.*
- *For further guidance, see page 27.*

Question 1(d) – the analysis and evaluation of the utility of a source

SOURCE D

One of the success stories of post-devolution Wales was the exceptionally high level of representation achieved by women in the National Assembly. Following the elections of May 2003, women constituted 50 per cent of the membership of the Assembly, the highest proportion of women's representation in the world.

Geraint H. Jenkins, an historian writing in his book A Concise History of Wales (2007)

(d)   How useful is Source D to an historian studying the success of women AMs in the National Assembly for Wales?

[6 marks]

- *Aim to concentrate upon three focus areas – content, origin and purpose.*
- *Remember to refer to how useful the source is to the historian.*
- *For further guidance, see page 72.*

Question 1(e) – explain differences in interpretation

SOURCE E

There were three stages in the emancipation of women:

The first was the long campaign of propaganda and organisation, at the centre of which ... stood Dame Millicent Fawcett.

The second was the campaign of the militants (the Suffragettes).

The third was war.

... without the [work of] ... Dame Millicent Fawcett and her colleagues, neither militancy nor the War could have produced the crop [result].

From an article entitled 'A Great Reformer' in The Guardian *on 6 August 1929*

SOURCE F

It was women's contribution to the war effort by working on the land, in factories, in all sorts of jobs at home and with the troops that made certain they would be granted the vote.

... The sight of women doing all kinds of 'men's work' had challenged traditional ideas and stereotypes about women. This made it much harder for the opponents of women's suffrage to argue that they were not capable of voting responsibly.

Alex Brodkin and other historians writing in the textbook OCR GCSE History B: Modern World *(2009)*

(e)   Why do Sources E and F have different views about why women were granted the vote in 1918?

[8 marks]

- *You must comment upon both sources, in each case referring to the content and the author.*
- *Remember to explain why the two sources have different views.*
- *For further guidance, see page 42.*

These examples are taken from Section B of the examination and deal with the changing experience of women at home in Wales and England from 1900 to the present day.

Question 2(b) – the understanding of a key feature through the selection of appropriate knowledge

(b)   Describe how labour-saving devices have changed work in the home since the 1960s.

[5 marks]

- *You will need to describe at least two key features.*
- *Be specific and avoid generalised comments.*
- *For further guidance, see page 86.*

Question 2(c) – the selection of knowledge and the understanding of key features

(c)   i) Explain why many women had to make ends meet during the 1930s.

[4 marks]

ii) Explain why improvements in standards of housing have helped to change life for women in recent times.

[4 marks]

- *Remember to give a variety of reasons.*
- *Give specific details such as names, dates, events, organizations, and activities.*
- *For further guidance, see page 103.*

Question 2(d) – using your own knowledge to construct a two-sided essay

(d)   How successful have developments in home and family life been in changing the role of women from 1900 to the present day? Explain your answer fully.

[10 marks]

You should give a two-sided answer to this question:
  - discuss developments that brought about successful changes in the role of women;
  - discuss developments that resulted in only limited success;
and give a judgement.

- *Remember to use the scaffold. It is a useful writing frame, which gives you a steer about what to write about.*
- *Aim to link your paragraphs, covering a variety of key issues.*
- *You must provide a conclusion that is linked back to the question.*
- *For further guidance, see page 116.*

Glossary

auxiliary services	reserve or support services
bailey	the yard outside a house
bilateral schools	schools with separate streams for grammar and secondary modern pupils
census returns	the results of a census, which is a questionnaire sent to all householders
co-habitation	living together when not married
compliant	willing to do as they are told
comptometer	a person (or machine) who works with numbers
Conciliation Committee	a committee formed in 1910 to consider giving the vote to women
contributory system of insurance	a system where contributions are taken directly from people's wages
domestic ideology	the idea that the best role for a woman was that of raising a family and looking after the home
domestic service	working as a servant in a large house
empowering	a feeling of power and control over a situation
energy-efficient	use as little energy as possible
enfranchised	having the right to vote
feminism	the belief that women are treated unfairly and that society should be changed to create equality between the sexes
glass ceiling	an invisible barrier that prevents people from reaching the more powerful jobs
hierarchy	a certain order of importance
hire-purchase	paying for goods in parts as a monthly rent until they are fully paid for
kibbutz	a collective community in Israel that is based on agriculture
labour exchanges	these were similar to modern-day job centres
lady's maid	maid responsible for looking after the lady of the house
landed gentry	rich people who own land
maiden speech	first official speech in office
marriage bar	a law stating that women had to resign from work when they married
maternal mortality	mothers dying in childbirth
meteorologist	someone who studies and predicts the weather
modern housecraft	the modern way to look after the house and home
munitionettes	women munitions workers
oral testimony	evidence that has been given verbally
over and under houses	houses built on a slope with a door leading out from the upper storey, where one family lived, at the front at one level; and a door, where another family lived, leading out at the back, at the lower level
philanthropic	someone who is benevolent and charitable
pithead baths	washing facilities at the head of the coal mines

positive discrimination	taking into account factors such as gender or race in order to benefit groups that are under-represented
pre-fabs	pre-fabricated houses – these were built in factories before being transported to the appropriate site and put together
prevalence of diseases	many diseases were widespread
preventative health measures	ways to prevent people getting ill in the first place
pro-feminist	someone who believes in equality for women and campaigns for women's rights
reconstruction programme	a programme to rebuild the country's economy after the war
seasonal work	work that is only available at certain times of the year
smallholder	someone who owns a small farm
still room maid	a maid that worked in the room where the drinks and jams were made
suffrage	a view that is expressed by voting
the scholarship /11+ examination	an exam for eleven years olds to gain entry into grammar school
two-up, two-down houses	houses with just two rooms upstairs and two rooms downstairs
umbrella organization	one large organization that covers many smaller ones
unsanitary	not clean or hygienic
women's suffrage	votes for women